RELENTLESS

Empowering Stories of Overcoming Adversity

Dr. Nelson Beltijar, Visionary Author

Onyx Expressions Publishing

New Jersey

Copyright © 2023 Nelson Beltijar, PhD (h.c.)

Visionary Author

Cover Design by Mae Cervantes, Maegnetic Socials

All rights reserved. No part of this publication may be reproduced, distributed, or transmitted in any form or by any means, including scanning, photocopying, recording, or other electronic or mechanical methods, without the prior written permission of the publisher, except in the case of brief quotations embodied in reviews and certain other non-commercial uses permitted by copyright law.
If you would like permission to use material from this book (for other than review purposes), please contact the authors.

Thank you for respecting the authors' rights.

ISBN: 978-1-959061-11-3

What People Are Saying About
RELENTLESS...

Dr. Nelson Villaluz Beltijar, Congratulations on Being the Visionary Author of "Relentless : Empowering Stories of Overcoming Adversity !!!" - Keep spreading "FAITH" out Into the World with Your / Our "Story" - We're so Proud of You !!!
-
Sincerely, **Gregorio Hierco Beltijar** - (RIP Dec 16, 2020 Dad) - and - **Corazon Villaluz Beltijar** (Mom) & **Elaine Beltijar** (Sister)

Thank you so much for being such a "Resilient & Integrity" filled role model Ninong (God-Father) !!! - We Win !!!

Love, Awesome Austin
(Canada)

Chapter One, by Jim Zias, sets the tone for your entire "Relentless" reading experience. This is an Amazing book filled with uplifting co-authored Stories of "Overcoming" - You won't be disappointed.

Bobby Tossios
(Canada)

This heartfelt book takes you on a journey filled with strong emotions of loss, hope, and love. We witness the authors unwavering determination to rebuild their lives, leaving us deeply moved and inspired. Highly recommend it. The highlight of the book for me was "Chapter 11" by Dawn Long.

Louise Henline

The Journey of Winning and Losing by Tessa Gordon is a true testament that perseverance and self-love are building blocks to help overcome disappointments in life. Her testimony is aspiring and a great reminder to never give up on your vision, hopes and dreams!

Denise E
Toronto, Ontario

I love this book, especially Jay "Flex" Mark's story – truly inspiring for anyone dealing with adversity.

Dex

One of the reasons I enjoyed this book so much is that it highlights the resilience of the human spirit. We all face challenges and obstacles in life, but it's inspiring to see how people can dig deep, overcome their struggles, and emerge stronger on the other side just like co-author Sid Owsley did.

Yesh Yonash

Lindsay Cruz took a risk by not taking the traditional route to achieve her goals. Despite the hindrances that she has had in life, she continues to strive for success not just to fulfill her dreams but to also help other families fulfill their own. Lindsay has inspired us to not be afraid to start again and to manifest the life that we dream of. You'll see what I mean when you read her chapter.

Renz De Lara
IT Technician
(Canada)

Franklin Kington's chapter is not just a story about his adventures, it also highlights how he learned from his close calls. He faced challenges, gained knowledge and learnt a lot. He made choices and discovered the power within himself. Franklin shows us through his words that even when things are tough, we can find a way to make our lives better. His story teaches us to be strong, never give up, and always believe in ourselves. It's a chapter that will inspire you to think about your own life experiences and the lessons you might learn from them.

Lisa Marie Igbinovia

Primary Teacher, Parent Mentor, Speaker, Artist and Children's Book Illustrator
www.XquizitLearners.co.uk https://linktr.ee/Xquizitlearners

This book is not only encouraging and uplifting, it is reassuring and transparent. These are real people who have shared raw and emotional journeys that would resonate with anyone who's ever been through anything in life that left you feeling like you hit rock bottom. Hope and Promise ... is what you need and what you will feel with this book in your hands. I can relate all too well with Michael Clayborn's chapter 10. I appreciate his candor, because sometimes it's just hard to put into words. It's an easy read, and great reminder that even in life's lowest valleys, there is always a path of escape and recovery."

Anonymous

The different ways people overcome adversity and triumph are both fascinating and enlightening. This collection of personal experiences covers a variety of these journeys. Ly Smith's is especially eye-opening as it comes from a place so normal to so many of us. Seeming to "have it all" from the outside but missing something on the inside. The difference is Mrs. Smith did something about it. She looked both inside herself and outside herself to find what she was seeking. And she found it both places.

It's inspiring how she is now helping others do what she did. Keep helping us matter.

Jeff Klein
757-96-SPEAK (77325)
Schedule a Visit Here: https://calendly.com/visitwjeff
Find Speakers at www.SpeakerCoop.com
Behind the Lectern Podcast: http://tiny.cc/jeffpod
Download Free Business Speaking Education:
www.SpeakerCoop.com/Education
Download Free Business Networking
Education:https://jeffkleinspeaker.com/education/

An inspiring book about overcoming adversity. I was particularly taken by the chapter written by Briar Munro, a young woman who found herself trapped in a domestic violence relationship grappling with feelings of shame, and faced with life and death decisions about her future. Her story is both relatable and inspiring, as she finds her way back to a meaningful life full of possibility.

Kate W.

I found this book very helpful in terms of advancing my financial literacy. In particular, Karl Davidson's chapter opened my eyes to the wider factors around wealth creation. Karl's explanation around how time, energy and environment can impact our ability to create financial success was game changing for me. Karl provides practical, helpful tips that anyone can implement. Karl has helped me to expand my money mindset.

I would highly recommend this book to everyone, it is packed full of information that is accessible to all. Karl's knowledge and wisdom shines through on the pages. Well worth a read.

Gillian MacGann, Wellness Coach, Founder of Life Expansion Coaching

My child's perspective on work-life balance was an emotional journey and filled my heart with pride and joy. Exploring the complexities of work-life balance while sharing personal experiences as a devoted parent and ambitious professional reminded me of my own struggles. I couldn't be prouder of Justin Smith's achievement in writing this thought-provoking and heartfelt chapter.

Balla Smith
Justin's Mom

La Toya Bond, I loved your chapter. It breaks my heart you had to write it, but only you could write such a powerful story. Speaking of Love, yours and your father's to each other and the community you shared as a family your biological one and the family you two enveloped in love. I'm so proud of you.

Mrs. Wilton

Wow! What an inspirational read! Reading "The Journey of Winning by Losing" by Tessa Gordon was so heartfelt. It takes courage to relocate your life from another country with nothing but faith and never giving up. I will live by D.R.O.P.

BK
Canada

This book is about 21 people, each sharing their personal story of heartbreak and adversity. But what's different about this book is that each of these individuals were able to overcome their personal tragedy and create something positive to help other people.

The chapter that resonated with me the most was Karan MacLaren's and her story about the loss of her child.

This is a parent's worst nightmare, and tears stung my eyes as she shared her journey through grief, guilt and sorrow.

As with each of these authors, Karan is changed by her loss and she decides to honour her child with a lifetime of giving back in her own unique way.

Truly an inspirational story.

Brad McCrorie
Chef & Author

Very well written, Very Inspirational - Loved Aubrey Johnson's Chapter : "The Lowest Point In My Life"

Tonya Johnson

"We are so proud of our son Jim Zias! His courage, his love of helping others is only equal by his willingness to never, ever give up. His amazing chapter in this wonderful book shows he's grown up to be the man we raised him to be!"

We love you,
Bill and Jeannie Zias

Lindsay Cruz's chapter is proof that it's possible to "restart" chasing one's dreams regardless of their age, setbacks, and circumstances. It's amazing what one can accomplish when they turn their brain on and commit to succeeding no matter what. Enjoy my older Sister's Chapter : "Life Is A Series Of Thin Threads".

Allyanna Cruz
Medical Administration
(Canada)

Flex Marks has an Inspiring story with a great message of overcoming obstacles and helping others.

Bob Hanson

Co-Author Frankie Kington turned his life around from mixing with the wrong crowd to becoming an Entrepreneur. He shows Courage and Bravery and is a fine example of a thought leader who wants to help Troubled youth.

Roger Bertrand
Public Speaker - Writer & Poet

This book was amazing. I enjoyed reading about the obstacles faced and how they were overcome. My favorite chapter was chapter 10 by Michael Clayborn. My dad is brave for finding strength to share his story. I'm proud to call you my father! Let's Go!

Malachi

I bought this book because my friend Ly Smith is one of the contributing authors. I'm grateful she has shared her story more fully with this reading audience. I've heard Ly speak a few times, and I appreciate knowing even more of her story.

The other authors are also inspiring in their messages and I'm grateful I bought the book.

Jackie Bailey
International Conversation Coach for Kids | The Speak Feed Lead Project
https://jackiebailey360.com/
425-503-5954

~~~~~~~~~~~~~~~~~~~~~~~~~~~~~~~~~~

Very inspiring. This book is full of inspiring stories but the chapter that stuck with me the most was from contributor, Briar Munro. She handled the very challenging subject matter of domestic abuse thoughtfully and honestly. I was so inspired by her journey.

Lia M

~~~~~~~~~~~~~~~~~~~~~~~~~~~~~~~~~~

I bought the Kindle version from Karl Davidson, and am waiting for the hard copy. Definitely a book for the reading shelf at home. This book has been very insightful into working smarter and not harder. Karl's wisdom and knowledge regarding financial education has helped me to level up and structure out a diversified portfolio. I knew about the importance of energy but did not understand about the impact the environment had on one's self until I read this book. I highly recommend this book.

Darren McKevitt, Author & CEO/Founder of McKevitt's Elite Coaching and Hypnotherapy

www.darrenmckevitt.com

~~~~~~~~~~~~~~~~~~~~~~~~~~~~~~~~~~

Wow, Justin Smith's chapter really struck a chord. I also balance being a dad and a professional, so his take on work-life balance hit close to home. A must-read for any parent.

Ben Smith
Justin's Brother
Operations Manager, Simply Smart Home
simplysmarthome.ca

Your effort to help other people in your own time of suffering is remarkable La Toya. The chapter was written with love and you can feel the love. I also like the fact that you did not allow your father to die in vain. He will now be remembered for the man he was.

Keith

I've known Dr. Nelson Beltijar for over 20 years now. He's a Huge supporter of those that are In his Life and I can Honestly say that I've Witnessed him leave his mark Everywhere he goes, creating a trail of Legendary & Memorable stories Along the Way that will eventually Outlive even Him. With his anthology, "Relentless : Empowering Stories Of Overcoming Adversity" by Your side, you Will be Reminded that there's Nothing you Can't Handle. Do your "Souls" a Favour and Purchase a Copy of this book "Today" !!!

Adam Lang
Managing Director, Juniper Park\TBWA Canada
(Canada)

~~~~~~

This book is a must read for anyone who is looking for encouragement to continue on, stay the course, and make it to the other side of their challenges. I especially enjoyed Aubrey Johnson's Chapter 4. His message of living through his lowest moments is so relatable, as well as, a reminder that we all can overcome adversity when we believe in ourselves and the power of change.

Jimmy IV
Creator & Host of the SexyCoolLoungepodcast

~~~~~~

To our Dad and my Husband,
"We have always believed in you Jim Zias, thank you for your devotion to those you love! You are an inspiration and we are so blessed to have you in our lives. Your steadfastness in the face of challenges is who you are, what a story!"

Love Youuuu,
Your soulmate Helen and your little girls, Zoe and Victoria

What a great book! Very inspirational! Great for seeking growth or gaining strength through other people's adversity stories. Love chapter 12 by Flex Marks.

Anel R.

~~~~~~

Lindsay Cruz's chapter is proof that it's possible to "restart" chasing one's dreams regardless of their age, setbacks, and circumstances. It's amazing what one can accomplish when they turn their brain on and commit to succeeding no matter what. Enjoy my older Sister's Chapter : "Life Is A Series Of Thin Threads".

Allyanna Cruz
Medical Administration
(Canada)

~~~~~~

Master Gordon's story leaves me wanting to read more. With only $100 in her pocket, how did she build her business and her new life? Tessa is a champion and a winner who has earned her success. I want to hear her story!

Patty Retsinas

~~~~~~

Frankie Kington has such a wonderful story of how you can turn your life around. In fact, I read the entire anthology book in one day !!! - (I couldn't put it down) - I would highly recommend this book to anybody who feels that they are not succeeding in life and not reaching their full potential. Frankie's bravery & resilience is displayed in overcoming the 9 obstacles he had to face & overcome in his life.

Melanie Worthington
Musician and Piano Teacher

"Chapter 10" of this book is incredible and the first thing I reflected on was, wow the author really made sense of his experience and challenges better than he thought he did. The chapter that I'm talking about was written by Michael Clayborn, who is actually my dad. Loving and a kind dad. And no, I am not rating this a five star because it's my dad, but in general the chapter was inspiring to me.

xoxo - "Gabby"

Incredible read - brave, honest, and heartwarming. The whole book is amazing. I was particularly drawn to Briar Munro's chapter. It is an important story to be told so that others don't feel so alone or thinking it is their fault. Thank you all for sharing your stories about bravery, being relentless and overcoming adversity.

Jane

Reading my partner's story was a deeply personal experience. His heartfelt exploration of work-life balance resonated with me on many levels, as I live it too! I am incredibly proud of Justin Smith's attempt to positively impact parents who are searching for a harmonious blend of work and family life. Well done, my love !

Anna Smith
Justin's Wife
Owner, Bloom Beauty Studio

The chapter tribute to your dad was well-written, sad, and hopeful. You did an amazing job La Toya Bond. Thank you for your courage.

Carmela

All the stories in this book are relatable and empower me to fight through adversity. I read Tessa Gordon's story to my 9-year-old daughter and she loved that the word "Can't" was not allowed. She also loved that this story was coming from a Black woman like herself. She saw herself reflected in Tessa and the challenges she too faces as she tries to navigate her current challenges with school. A MUST READ!

MK

Never Underestimate the Heart of a Champion !!! - The lived Experiences of Each contributor will Inspire you to be a Powerful and Relentless force. Dr. Nelson Beltijar represents the Strength and Spirit that Drives individuals to Excel and accomplish Extraordinary feats.

John Tsagarelis
Portfolio Manager / Lawyer
(Canada)

Great book and great contributors to the content ! Aubrey Johnson's story in Chapter 4 was the highlight of the book ! Highly recommend it !

Jay Johnson
District Manager at Extra Space Storage
(www.ExtraSpace.com)

"My Brother, My Brother-in-law, and My Uncle. We knew that your chapter would help propel Relentless: Empowering Stories of Overcoming Adversity to an International Number One Best Seller! Your faith and optimism, and dedication and determination have always been available to loved ones that surround you!

We are so blessed to call you ours Jim Zias!

Love,
Mary, Lu and Sammy

There are many inspiring stories in this book but the Flex Marks chapter was my favorite. A great story of a man who was dealing with his own health issues while also being an amazing friend to someone who was dealing with the biggest battle of their life. A great story of adversity and strength.

Cassie

~~~~~~

Frankie Kington's story is Engaging & Encouraging !!! Until we make a conscious decision to change the course of our lives it will never change. Frankie clearly conveys this in his Chapter : "A Cat with Nine Lives". Frankie shared incidents from his life like getting into fights, using illegal dangerous drugs, and how one decision changed the course of his life for the better. Frankie's story is motivating and breathes hope !!!

Jomer De Leon
Life Coach & Fitness Coach

~~~~~~

Before You Quit ... READ THIS BOOK"

Relentless: Empowering Stories of Overcoming Adversity is a MUST READ! The transparency and vulnerability of each author lets us know that we are not alone, and that it is possible to Overcome Adversity.

One such Author is Michael Clayborn. Through his story, "This Push is for You, Momma," he allowed us to see and feel everything connected to losing a parent AND how to deal with the aftermath. Michael's story is one I have watched replayed countless times with men in my own family and in my community. However, he has allowed us to take a peek into how he navigated the grief process, how he got the help he needed, and how he was able to move forward. If you are dealing with any kind of grief, allow Michael Clayborn's story to give you hope!

RELENTLESS ... is full of stories that uplift and inspire. So, if you're feeling like throwing in the towel, DON'T! This book may be just what you need to pick yourself up, brush yourself off, and try again!"

Traci Logan

~~~~~~

When she reached the end of her rope, she tied a knot and hung on for her own happiness. In reading Briar Munro's story, it was inspiring to see a light at the end of a long, dark tunnel. Even though she overcame serious health issues, requiring surgery to accomplish skills in dance and martial arts, it was frightening to hear how self-doubt invited the horrors of a misleading man into her life. When you want to embrace the best in everyone, sometimes you are fooled by hidden deceit. Briar rose above the challenges she faced and chose the right time on that fork in the road. By making good and educated decisions, she can speak with a voice of authority and encouragement to help others climb out of their despair. This is a rewarding story to be shared for hope to return. Thanks for the message, Briar.

Deb Dorsey

~~~~~~

Justin Smith's story is relatable and empowering, leaving parents with a renewed sense of determination to navigate life's challenges. I recommend this chapter to anyone (not just parents) seeking inspiration and guidance in finding their own balance.

Dan Demsky
CEO @ Unbound Merino
unboundmerino.com

Tessa Gordon's journey to fulfill her purpose is truly inspirational. Her genuine desire to see people elevate regardless of their situation is fundamental to her success. She reminds us of the power of believing in ourselves and being aligned with God's plan for our lives.

~ Cheryl E, Toronto ON

If you've Struggled through Tough times, or Know anyone who Currently is, I highly Recommend this Book. It's Powerful in Every way. Yes ! - Yes !! - and - YES !!! - I really Related, as many Will, to the Co-Authored Stories within "Relentless : Empowering Stories Of Overcoming Adversity". Dr. Nelson Beltijar teaches Us so much about personal Strength and How us Humans can Overcome almost Anything.

Eilona Skvirsky
Recording Artist & Fashion Influencer
(USA)

Jim Zias, Your narration of this incredible struggle to overcome the odds was so encouraging to read. I thank you so much, and like I remember you having always said, the best is yet to come!"

Winning! Winning! Winning!

Your friend,
Manuel Goldstein

Frankie Kington writes the story of his childhood and early adulthood in an easy-to-read and conversational style. He had many difficult challenges growing up and veered into a self-destructive path as a young adult. He tells you the story of how he turned his life around with compassion and honesty. It is an excellent chapter for anyone wanting motivation to move forward from a tough place to a better place. The wisdom and compassion that Frankie brings to the telling of the story is inspiring.

Debbie Esplin
Cook & Healer

"Let's just say this book was well thought out and put together as the masterpiece it is. Co-author, Michael Clayborn's story is phenomenal and hits home to the core. The strength of a lion is what I get when I read the pages of Michael's story. I too have faced adversity such as Michael's but was reminded by his words " There is no problem you face in life that isn't already designed for you to win". Michael, you are phenomenal and you're an inspiration to many. Keep sharing your testimony because someone is being helped."

Your Queen, Porsha

~~~~~~~~~~~~~~~~~~~~~~~~~~~~~~~~

Justin Smith's chapter was an inspiring journey. I felt empowered and encouraged after reading it, and I know others will too. Congratulations on being a part of a fantastic book !

Nate Kogan
Freelance Graphic Designer

~~~~~~~~~~~~~~~~~~~~~~~~~~~~~~~~

D.R.O.P. - Discipline, Respect, Open-Mindedness and Positivity will be at the forefront of my everyday living. Tessa Gordon's story can motivate anyone who reads it. Her determination to teach Tae Kwon Do to anyone without being limited by their ability, is the definition of a true Master.

MM
Toronto, Canada

~~~~~~~~~~~~~~~~~~~~~~~~~~~~~~~~

We Are so Proud of our daughter, Lindsay Cruz, for displaying Creative Resilience when it comes to going after her Goals & Dreams. Instead of surrendering her ambitions because of untimely, yet exciting circumstances, she chose to grow into the person that she needed to become in order to professionally succeed in a new country that she, and we, call home today !!! - I'm sure many of you may see yourselves within her story of deflating challenges & eventual personal victory.

Nelson and Olivia Cruz
Parents
(Philippines / Canada)

~~~~~~

Your Chapter reminds us all that it's "POSSIBLE" to overcome "Adversity" - I witnessed it, I lived it alongside you, and now I and / or We all "Get" a chance to become Inspired & Motivated by Your documented Resilience within the Pages of This book. Congratulations to you Dr. Nelson "The People's Champ" Beltijar & your Relentless Co-Authors !!! - We Love You Brother !!!

Dennis Ducusin & Family
Modeify Hair
(Canada)

~~~~~~

Inspiring, uplifting, encouragement. Reading a part of Tessa Gordon's life journey for sure, will inspire endless souls as to follow your inner spirit. A powerhouse of strengthen endurance. I encourage all to read. Beautifully written. I would love to see more of her work. Bravo.

Jackie Barrett

~~~~~~

Truly inspiring and necessary reading !!! - "Relentless: Empowering Stories of Overcoming Adversity" is a book that has touched my heart and changed the way I see life. It's filled with amazing stories from different authors who have faced tough challenges and come out stronger.

This book is honest, real, and inspiring. The authors share their personal struggles, showing us that no obstacle is too big and that we can grow and empower ourselves through tough times.

What makes "Relentless" special is how it connects with readers. As I read the stories, I felt inspired and motivated to apply the same type of mental resilience into my own life.

I highly recommend this book, and Sid Owsley's written chapter "Persistently Determined, to anyone looking for inspiration and empowerment. It's a game-changer that shows us our circumstances don't define us and that we have the strength to overcome anything.

George Levy

~~~~~~

Nit Sua was the youngest Co-Author within our Anthology and his chapter was titled : "It's All About Perspective". Although he was only "12 years old" at the time, you'll see that he's living proof that "Wisdom" can be acquired at any age. Thank you for saying "Yes" to being a Part of this Project Nit Sua !!! - Know that I'm extremely Proud of you and I can't wait to Meet, and "Introduce", the Man that You'll grow up to become in "2028" - Until then, stay Focused, love People, stay Driven, remain Humble, and most of all ... Be "Relentless" - #GloryToGod

Dr. Nelson Beltijar Ph.D, h.c - (3x Amazon # 1 International Best Selling Book Author) • Coach • Speaker • Visionary Author • Friend - (Canada) - www.ThePositiveDrip.com

Disclaimer

Please be advised that the information in this book is not meant to replace the advice of a certified professional. The content of this book is for informational purposes only and makes no guarantees concerning the level of success you may experience by following the advice or strategies offered. Please consult a licensed advisor in matters relating to your personal and professional well-being including your mental, emotional and physical health, finances, business, legal matters, family planning, education, and spiritual practices.

The views and opinions expressed throughout this book are those of the individual author and do not necessarily reflect the views or opinions of any other agency, organization, employer, publisher, or company.

If you choose to attempt any of the methods mentioned in this book, the author and publisher advise you to take full responsibility for your safety and well-being. The author and publisher are not liable for any damages or negative consequences for any result, action, or preparation to any person reading or following the information in this book. The author and publisher assume no responsibility for errors, inaccuracies, omissions, or any other inconsistencies herein.

The use of this book implies the readers' acceptance of this disclaimer and his/her agreement to discharge the publisher and author from any and all claims or causes of action, known or unknown, arising out of the contents of this book.

DEDICATION

This Anthology is Dedicated to ALL of My Relentless Global Brothers & Sisters Who Have Faced, Overcame, and Learned From "Adversity."

Additionally, this Book is Dedicated to my Selfless, Loving, and Brave Parents: Mr. Gregorio Hierco Beltijar (RIP2020) and Mrs. Corazon Villaluz Beltijar - Thank you both for "Everything" !!!
- Without You, I Am Nothing.

Love Always - Your Dear Boy,
Dr. Nelson Beltijar - (The People's Champ)

Ps - Honourable mention: Elaine Beltijar, my brilliant sister, and last but not least, Awesome Austin.

TABLE OF CONTENTS

1: Winning By Jim Zias 2

2: It Takes A Little More By Dr. John E. Gray 14

3: Free To Be Me By Briar Munro 26

4: The Lowest Point In My Life By Aubrey Johnson 36

5: This Candy Is Good For You By Ly Smith 46

6: The Difference In Thinking By Karl Davidson 57

7: Love, Loss, & Divine Purpose By Karan Maclaren 69

8: A Cat With Nine Lives By Frankie Kington 79

9: The Journey Of Winning By Losing By Master Tessa Gordon 87

10: This Push Is For You, Momma By Michael Clayborn 95

11: Breaking The Cycle: Empowering Women To Find Their Path To Redemption By Dawn Long 104

13: Life Is A Series Of Thin Threads By Lindsay Cruz 121

14: Work/ Life Balance Is Bullsh*T By Justin Smith 128

15: Castle In The Sand By Meaghan Tanaka 136

16: My Hardest Battle, My Unseen Blessing By Tony Lynch 146

17: Persistently Determined By Sid Owsley 152

18: Building Resilience In The Face Of Adversity By Benitha Samuel 160

19: It's All About Perspective By Nit Sua 169

20: Speaking Of Love By La Toya Bond 179

21: When "Adversity" Attacks: Conquer Or Crumble ??? By Dr. Nelson Beltijar *188*

About The Project Manager, ... *225*

Connect With Our Writing Consultant Dr. Angie Gray *227*

About The Publisher *228*

ACKNOWLEDGMENTS

Cover Design by Mae Cervantes, Maegnetic Socials

Project Management by Dr. Angie Gray

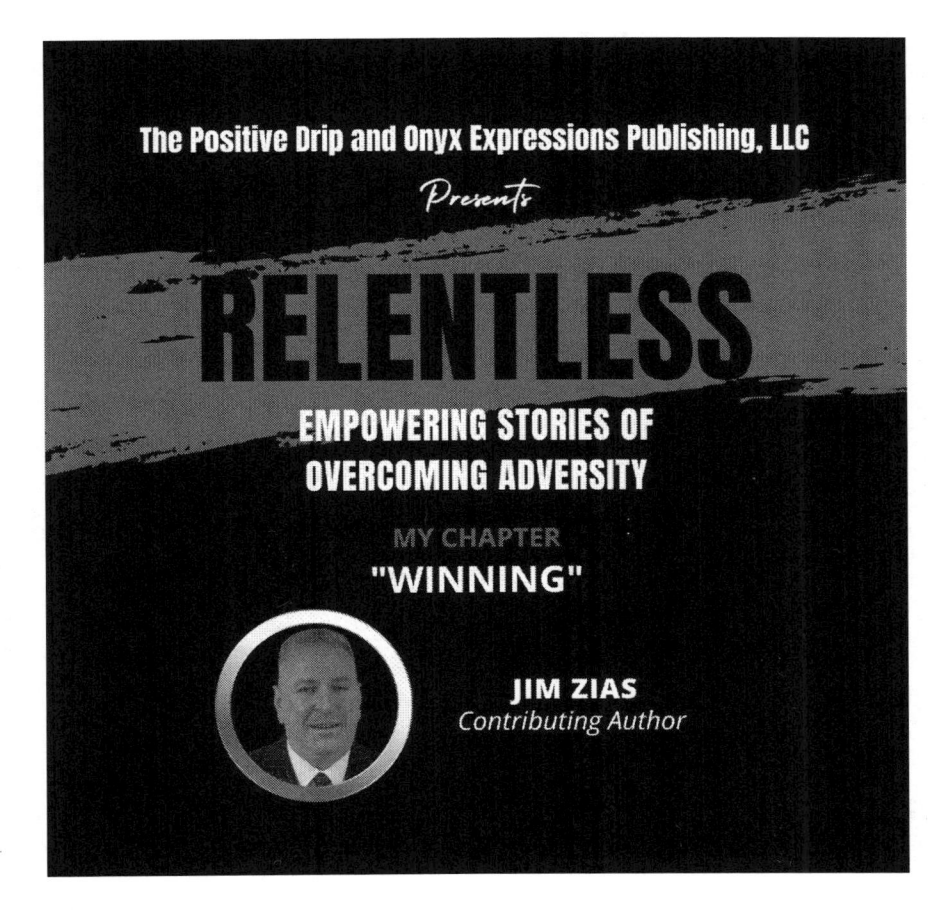

The Positive Drip and Onyx Expressions Publishing, LLC

Presents

RELENTLESS

EMPOWERING STORIES OF OVERCOMING ADVERSITY

MY CHAPTER
"WINNING"

JIM ZIAS
Contributing Author

1: Winning

By Jim Zias

One afternoon in late June...
He had messaged me over the last few weeks, saying that he hadn't been feeling well. I wasn't concerned, he had always been the type of person that would burn the midnight candle, always on the go, full of energy, he would cut corners now and then with regards to shut eye. Running his own practice, spending time with his family and friends, contributing to the community, it was understandable.

The messages kept coming in over the last few weeks, "I'm not feeling well..."

One afternoon in late June 2016, while lying alone on my teenage daughter's bed, enjoying the cool breeze coming through the window overlooking the valley, I received a message that would leave me changed forever...

I heard my familiar text notification, "ding!" With my less than 20/20 vision I raised my iPhone to read the message. I glimpsed sight of one of the most terrifying words in the English language, "cancer".

My mind immediately began to race, I put the phone down praying I didn't see the word I thought I just saw, and my breathing began to pick up, my heart beating ever faster, I took a deep breath to muster the courage to pick up my iPhone again and read the text again.

"The doctor called me about my tests, I have cancer"

I went into denial, is it April Fools' Day? Who makes an April fool's Day joke about cancer? Are you sure the text is from him? How can this be?

I descended into a full-blown panic attack, my heart was pounding out of my chest, I was hyperventilating...

I began to pray, God please, this can't be real.

I pulled myself together to read his text one final time.

My brother just informed me he's been diagnosed with cancer.

The Visit

Devastated, I broke the news to my wife Helen, she had always adored him, and in 2016 they had been friends almost 35 years, she immediately broke down.

A few days later, after finding out the name of the hospital he had just been admitted to, I went to visit him, I still didn't believe it... I had to see him there with my own eyes.

When I arrived at the hospital, the first thing I was taken back by was how pale and lifeless the hallways looked. Gray and pale green, the whole place resonated with sorrow and a kind of hopelessness. It felt like a prison more than a hospital. I asked for directions to the room where he had been admitted to at the front desk and made my way up to the floor.

I made my way to the room that I was led to, and I saw him lying there, I swear I didn't know if he was dead or alive.

The only word I could think of to say was "Eh!"

He didn't open his eyes, he didn't turn his head, he simply made a small sound when his lips moved.

He was on death's door…

Our mother was there, just sitting in the corner, her eyes lit up when she saw me. My heart broke for her.

At that moment, and only at that moment, I believed…

WAR

I have an expression for the last 12 years of my life, the darkest years of my life.

"Life is War and War is Life"

The amount of sorrow, grief, heartbreak, suffering and adversity I had gone through was comical.

Death, sickness, death, sickness, death, death, near death and more Death. As of this writing, there have been over 25 funerals amongst my family and friends and heroes.

Most horrific of all was the death of a precious little boy. My nephew Billy Gabriel.

And now my brother on Death's Door?

Another battle had now begun, and the blast of the Shofar would be heard once again, it was time to go to War.

I have come to believe that the single most powerful force in the human soul is will.

Those who are victors, are victorious, because the possibility of losing simply doesn't exist for them. It's inconceivable.

There is only one possible outcome in their battle ...Winning.

That word became the mantra for a War that would go on for years.

"You're gonna win!"

THE MONTHS TO COME

He had to escape from that place. Unable to diagnose the type and specific location of the cancer, Dr. K drugged him up, tied him down, and left him to die. Our mom petitioned day and night to have him transferred downtown. Against all odds several weeks later she succeeded.

The downtown hospital was world class, and you knew that the moment you walked into the lobby.

There he would have a fighting chance, and within days Doctor B accurately diagnosed his cancer and began chemotherapy immediately. Doctor B was a General, all business, no emotion, a machine at War. He had an enemy to crush.

I would visit him several times per week over the summer of 2016, he never so much as ventured outside once to see a beautiful summer day. He chose not to. All the while I knew I had to help create a compelling future, a vision. For all the great quarterbacks in history marching down the field in the Super bowl, victory is almost always incremental, one first down at a time, a touchdown drive.

First down after first down, it was the only analogy I could think of to help him see a future where he wins.

He would just look outside his window and our mom would be by her boy's side every day, day in day out. Dad had suffered a stroke some years earlier and was limited in movement.

The General had ordered chemotherapy strikes five times a week for months, it almost killed him.

Watching him go through this almost killed me.

Eventually his hair began to fall out, mom called a cousin who was a barber, Dennis came down and shaved his head bald. I got the idea next time I got my hair cut to shave my head bald too.

SOLIDARITY

By fall the tide was beginning to turn. He was winning.

My youngest daughter Victoria, participated in the annual Terry Fox run at school, I took a short video clip of her after the run, "I'm running for you...!" she said in the clip, I sent it to him,

He texted back overjoyed and teary-eyed. "Thank you! "he replied.

THANKSGIVING, 2016

Thanksgiving was approaching and he made a request to come home for just the weekend to be with his family, inexplicably the General declined his request. That would mean he would miss one day of chemotherapy, Thanksgiving Monday. The General would not allow that.

At home with my family Thanksgiving Monday, we were wrapping up a truly beautiful day, driving my mom and dad home with a tray of leftover turkey and stuffing I suggested on a whim let's go by and surprise visit him in the hospital.

We did and we walked through the lobby, the place which had always reminded me of a beehive, buzzing with constant activity, looked like a ghost town. We made our way up to the 8th floor and walked into his room, there he was with our mom and sister Elaine, their eyes lit up when they saw us, it was a wonderful, perfect Thanksgiving Day celebration with all of us reunited together.

In the following weeks, we received the news that his cancer blood markers were plummeting, he was winning.

I began to share with him the dream of coming home for Christmas.

One snowy day in December the General made that dream come true.

We were all ecstatic, my oldest daughter Zoe accompanied me to the hospital for his grand exit out of that room where he had been a prisoner of war for many, many months.

Prior to his release, he received a stern warning from the General that if he ever started to cough, he must immediately 911 to the hospital, the common cold with his almost nonexistent immune system could kill him.

A few days later, he did begin to cough... he called me, and I said rush to the hospital immediately. He did.

Later, I went to grab something out of my car, walking down my front porch in the Canadian Arctic winter in my flip-flops and my iPhone in my right pocket, I got a call.

It was him. Luckily, my phone was where I could easily reach it. He was in sheer terror. The General placed him in what can only be described as the hermetically sealed isolation room in the basement of the hospital.

All by himself. Not another soul to be seen.

"Why are they doing this to me?!"

"Mom is only allowed to come down here if she's wearing an astronaut suit!!!" he screamed.

I tried to calm him, I told him he can't hurt you by overreacting like this, but he puts you in grave danger by under reacting and dismissing this.

The General was taking no chances.

Soon he was better,

A few days later my wife and our young girls flew off to New York City for a few days over Christmas time.

One magical moment while sitting in Bryant Park's Christmas market sipping a hot chocolate, you know with those little tiny marshmallows, I got a text.

They were letting him go.

He was going home for Christmas.

Reading that text, I let out a joyous Christmas cheer.

A few days before the New Year he told me that the doctors were now strongly suggesting major surgery to prevent the cancer from spreading in the future.

He chose the surgery, it was scheduled for on January 16, 2017

He texted me that morning at 5:32 AM telling me they were in a taxi headed down to the hospital for the surgery, I got up, grabbed a coffee, washed up and headed down there. We met in the surgery waiting room.

Our mom, our sister Elaine, and I were so uneasy that morning, suddenly the doors opened, and a small army of doctors and nurses burst out, confident and cheerful, they informed him it was time. Mom hugged and kissed her boy goodbye. We watched as they wheeled him away into the operating room.

The head surgeon, Dr. H finally came out and met with us and told us all had gone well. He was truly a remarkable man to be in the presence of. The surgery lasted almost 16 hours, and despite all of mom's pleas, they would not let her see her boy in the recovery room shortly after midnight on the morning of January 17. The next few hours would be critical.

A breaking weather alert warned of an oncoming ice storm, we decided it was best if we all went home and return the next morning.

The next day we walked into his hospital room, there he lay, breathing tubes down his mouth, an IV in his arm, he had made it, so far.

A few weeks later he recovered enough for them to release him.

WINNING

In April 2017, he was given the official declaration from the General himself, "your cancer is in remission, now go and create the conditions each day to stay cancer free"!

I sat silently praying in the waiting area, and when I heard the first few words of his voice while he was in the back speaking to the nurses, before

I could even lay eyes on him, I knew that my brother from another Mother Nelson Villlaluz Beltijar had won the Super Bowl of Life.

The next several years I would be driving countless times back-and-forth with Nelson to physiotherapy sessions and checkups in the downtown hospital core. Eventually, his recovery led to him abandoning his wheelchair and ultimately not needing his cane.

The Fall of next year, Sunday, September 30, 2018, we all participated in the CIBC Run for the Cure held at the University of Toronto downtown St. George campus.

We chose the 1K walk/run, as we approached the end Nelson asked me to stop the wheelchair we all were taking turns pushing him in. He daringly chose to walk the last 50 meters to the finish line entirely on his own.

All of us, full of anticipation and hope, watched courage in action.

Witnessing those last few steps, his beloved little nephew Austin cheering him on, was pure bliss.

Our friend Jay had his videographer friend Dex record and immortalize those final seconds crossing the finish line.

It has been said God works in mysterious ways.

Looking back years later, these were some of the most fulfilling and meaningful days of my life.

Reflecting on this incredible journey I was privileged to be a part of, I learned forever lessons about love, anguish, suffering, friendship and hope.

Hope is a good thing, maybe the best of things…

And no good thing ever dies... **"Never Surrender, never give up Hope, you're gonna Win!"**

~ About Jim Zias ~

Husband, father, brother, son, uncle, nephew, loyal friend, warrior, and godfather.

On this journey we call life, Jim Zias defined himself as a master strategist. He prides himself as being an individual who has found more meaning and fulfillment in serving others first, than himself. He holds onto the adage that it is truly more blessed to give than to receive.

Jim believes a life well-lived entails constantly learning and growing in knowledge and wisdom, and refusing to ever succumb to the concept of surrender.

Like all souls, he was born into a life of adversity and unending challenges. He describes his life experiences as being like pages in a book. He has found great joy in sharing with others, so that they may draw inspiration from his life story.

Perhaps the ultimate life lesson Jim has been taught is the following simple truth. ***Victory can only be found in perseverance.***

Jim reminds his readers that we are captivated by the need to know what lies ahead in our travels, while hoping to forecast what the coming years may bring us. However, he cautions, we know in our hearts that there is no true certainty in this life. When you inevitably walk through the valley of the shadow of death. Remember that you must never, ever, surrender, never lose hope, and that hope may be the greatest of things.

Your breakthrough, your sunrise, and your victory are just one more step away.

Jim resides in Toronto, Canada with his wife Helen, children Zoe and Victoria, and their dog Hope. Feel free to reach out to him anytime at JimZias@hotmail.com … and please put the word "Relentless" in the subject heading. Jim looks forward to connecting with you!

The Positive Drip and Onyx Expressions Publishing, LLC
Presents
RELENTLESS
EMPOWERING STORIES OF
OVERCOMING ADVERSITY
MY CHAPTER
"IT TAKES A LITTLE MORE"
DR. JOHN E. GRAY
Contributing Author

2:
It Takes A Little More

By Dr. John E. Gray

"**J**ust Do It.™" While this phrase has been trademarked since 1988 under the shoe company, Nike, as its slogan, it is more than just a slogan. It is a profound reminder to many, myself included, to simply buckle down and get to whatever task is in front of you. Unfortunately, I have often found myself to be a member of the "Procrastinators Anonymous Club of Elite Achievers." Now, obviously, this not an organization that I am a proud, card-carrying member, but nonetheless, it is true. I have achieved many things during my life's journey that weren't really feasible for me. You see, I wasn't born with many of the traditional things that most would consider to be advantageous. I didn't come from a family of affluence or great influence. I grew up in Newark, the largest city in New Jersey. The hood I call home, aka "Brick City," was ravaged by riots in 1967 and is, arguably, still trying to bounce back and recover over 50 years later. Affectionately named this because of its numerous housing projects, drugs, and violence, the place I call home, was not inherently a place where the concept of "Just Do It" could flourish and be the dominate way of life. That's a very eloquent way of saying, it was clear to me, from the very beginning that "Just Do It" was not exactly the slogan for my situation. That may work for some, but that wasn't going to work for me. "It's Going to Take a Little More," would have to be a mantra I'd have to adopt if I had any intention of thriving rather than just surviving. I borrowed that from the Champion brand athletic apparel slogan, *"It Takes a Little More to Make a Champion."* Though Champion has outfitted athletes for decades with sports apparel, it has become a little more than that for me. Let me explain; I was the youngest of nine children and my mother succumbed to breast cancer when I was just seven-years-old. As a ward of the State, stability was a bit elusive to me as I moved from foster home to foster home and group home to group home, with plastic trash bags housing all of my belongings. I say all of that to paint a clear picture for you...

Given my very humble beginnings, life has never been easy for me. The fact that you are reading this chapter right now, tells me something about you. I guessing that because you've decided to invest a few moments of your time with me, you can relate to my situation. The title of this chapter probably resonates with you because deep down inside, you know the things you are seeking to achieve are going to take a little more effort and a little more perseverance. Let's keep it real; like me, you have hopes and dreams to do more, be more and, have more. Sometimes just thinking about those things are overwhelming. This is only natural. I know you are doing your thing; making moves and making things happen, but I'm here to tell you that when you want to go to that next level it's going to take a little more. I always tell people that life will not pave a "Golden Road" for you simply because you have goals and good intentions. For years, I've watched our world being bogged down with problems and issues that seem impossible to fix. I know this may surprise you, but I've even had a few problems and issues of my own. The pandemic of 2020 and beyond, gave the world cause to pause. Like or not, we were forced to go to our collective corners and sit down for a minute. The covers and bandages were ripped off all kinds of problems and issues. Once hidden in plain sight, many ugly truths of the world were now exposed and made irrefutable even to those who had previously been able to turn a blind eye to or minimize because they were once only real and evident to the victims. During that time of isolation, I had plenty of time to reflect, reassess, regroup, and reset. I made a significant shift in my mindset. I heard it said that there are no problems in the world, but there are opportunities to find solutions. Trust me, life is going to give you every opportunity to show what you've got in terms of solutions. It's more about whether or not you choose to see it as a problem or as an opportunity to find a solution. I'm sure you may have accomplished this, that, or the other, but when you want to reach the pinnacle of what you really want, that C- Suite (or more like your See a Sweet goal - LOL) level goal, then it's going to take a little more. I believe we each can have, be, or do anything we want, but it's going to take a little more. I also believe there's a big difference between those who play in the game of life or simply watch it from the sidelines and those who decide to win the game and become champions of their own life. In fact, I believe we each have champion DNA within our blood. So, one day while I was taking a walk, it came to me that I wanted to be the champion I was called to be. As I pondered on this, I realized there is a recipe that a champion follows in order to tap into their true greatness... and from that my acronym for CHAMPION was born. Let me make this plain for you...

The C in **CHAMPION** is for **C**ourage. First, it's going to take a little more courage! It's going to take a little more courage to do the things that you want that are huge and are going to scare you. Don't worry, if they do scare you - they should scare you! If you're going after goals that are so easily attainable that you don't get butterflies in your stomach and you're not scared because of them, then you're not dreaming big enough. You have to reach higher - to the point that it scares you to death! Reach for those things that are going to test your faith because the only thing that can come out of it is a stronger sense of courage. In other words, get your courage up because life is going to challenge you and strengthen you. Life is going to throw punches at you to see what you are made of. As Mike Tyson said, "Everybody has a plan until they get punched in their mouth!"

The H in **CHAMPION** is for **H**unger. When it all boils down to the bare essence, being a champion starts with being hungry. It's going to take a little more hunger if you want to be great! Les Brown, one of the greatest motivational speakers ever, said "You've got to be hungry!" Unfortunately, there are those whose appetite don't match their goals! They're not hungry enough. You have to wake up thinking about this thing you say you want. You need to have your goal on your mind all day long. You've got to go to sleep thinking about this thing you want. You've got to wake up thinking about it. You've got to think about it all day long. You have to have a hunger pain! And then you've got to feed it with daily action. Just like you're physically hungry every day, you've got to be hungry enough to eat and act on it every day. Anybody that's ever been hungry knows I'm not talking about hungry just because you want a little snack. You have to be hungry for the full course meal of success, plus dessert!

I love watching zombie movies and my wife always asks me why I watch those crazy zombie movies. I watch because I see them as a microcosm of the human condition. People without ambition are walking around existing but they are not alive! They're not alive because they are not driven by their ambitions. You see, ambition feeds your purpose and your passion, and as I always say, "Your passion is your permission to pursue your purpose!" That's why ambition is so important because it is our inspirational compass. If you don't know where you're going, any road will lead you to nowhere! So, use ambition, passion, and purpose as your guides.

The A in CHAMPION is for **A**ttitude. To be honest attitude is one of the most important elements of a champion. Altitude and how far someone will go depends largely on their attitude. There are many layers of attitude as well. Attitude is essentially mindset. How one looks at various situations and circumstances determines their perspective. Their perspective is really their attitude about things. Do they view their situations and circumstances from a lens of positivity and determination or negativity and defeat? Do they recognize the part they play in their circumstances? Attitude also serves as a layer of accountability. In a sense, how one looks at the role they play in their own life relies heavily on if they are accountable for their actions. Do they take ownership for the part they could have done better or do they seek to find someone else to blame? Attitude is a power that we, and we alone, can control for ourselves. No one can "make" us see things from a certain viewpoint. Only we can decide to see things from a positive place or a negative place.

I would be remiss if I didn't also address the power that the attitude of gratitude gives to champions. When we choose to be grateful and look for the good in everything, our entire world shifts. There have been greats such as Napoleon Hill, Jim Rohn, etc. who have espoused the idea that what we focus on is what will dominate our lives. Do we focus on what we have and the positive or do we choose to focus on the negative and what we don't have? "Where our focus goes, our energy flows." I am reminded of the fable about the grandfather who teaching his grandson about good versus evil. In that story shares there are two wolves inside of each one of us who are fighting; one good and one evil. When the grandson asks him which one wins, the grandfather responds, "The one you feed." I think this story is so applicable here because for the champion it really is about which story or attitude does he feed the weak one or the strong one.

The M in CHA**M**PION is for **M**otivation. You need to have a little more motivation. Sadly, most people are only motivated when the "motivational cavalry" comes along to inject them with the motivation they need to get their "C-Suite" goals accomplished. In other words, they have to be motivated from some outside source. Now, don't get me wrong, it never hurts to get a dose of inspiration from greats such as Les Brown, Eric Thomas, or Tony Robbins. But, I'm here to tell it's going to take a little more. The greatest motivation you really need is an inside job. You have to want it bad enough to go get it. Whatever that it is for you, is for you if you decide to go get it. This inner motivation is called "internal locus of control." Many have of those who have an external locus of control never meet their C-Suite goals face-to-face. They allow them to be elusive, figments of their imagination which clearly don't serve them well. However, those with internal locus of control, are much more likely to achieve their goals and manifest their wildest dreams. With that in mind, you may be asking what exactly is a "locus of control." I'll keep it simple, but basically, "locus" of control, refers to the "location" of where one believes the series of actions and outcomes to produce their achievement happen. Those with an external locus look at achievement and fate from a position of luck, happenstance, or coincidence, suggesting that success is based solely on external forces. While those with an internal locus believe that their own inner forces control their fate, outcomes and actions. Well, I have to be honest, it takes both, some internal and external... but it's going to take a little more internal.

The P in CHAM**P**ION stands for **P**erseverance. Perseverance means that I'm unstoppable, and no matter what I endure I'm going to keep on keeping on! "Keep on keeping" on is a saying that we have in our culture and it can mean a whole lot of things, but when I say it in the context of this chapter, I want you to know exactly what it means. Keep on keeping on means that life is not going to play fair sometimes. Sometimes, despite our best intentions, life throws us a curveball or two. To persevere is to vow that you will keep fighting no matter the odds stacked against you. There is nothing more powerful than the human spirit, and there are times when that theory will be tested, but the resilient person whose life is dedicated to perseverance welcomes the challenges because they know that they will answer the call to fight for their goals and dreams. In the words of Malcolm-X, you've got to be willing to do whatever it takes, by any means necessary to go achieve your goals and dreams. Now, I am a champion, so I am referring only to those things in your own control and of course, legal. Please don't think that I'm suggesting anything that even remotely looks like underhandedness. I'm referring to putting in the necessary time, energy, and work. I don't want you to think that this is supposed to be easy - because it's not. Anything worth achieving is worth sacrifice and due diligence. In other words, it works if you work it!

The I in CHAMP**I**ON is for **I**nspiration. I have a few questions to ask. What inspires you? What moves you? In other words, what are you feeling in your Spirit that's going to propel you forward? If you're not living in a place of inspiration, what happens is it will ultimately dull your creativity. If it dulls your creativity, then it negatively impacts your productivity. In order to live in this constant state of inspiration, it becomes very important with whom you connect and why you choose to spend time with them. Did you know that sociological research says that we are the composite or sum total of our two to three closest friends? That adage, birds of a feather flock together, comes to mind because it turns out that according to that research I mentioned, it's not just an old wives' tale, it's pretty close to factual. With that in mind, I need you to take a critical look at your friends, friend groups, and associations to whom you give your time and energy. This is important because it's going to speak to who you really are at your core. When you look at them, you're looking at yourself! What I am saying is that if you hang around people who have no ambition... or if you hang around people with no vision... Well, I'm not actually going to say it here...that's a chapter for another book, but if you hang around people with creativity you're bound to become someone who is creative. If you spend time with those who are innovative and positive you're bound to pick up those traits and characteristics. Long story short, it's going to take a little more inspiration.

The O in CHAMPI**O**N is for **O**ptimism. Optimism means being able to see the forest and the trees; that you are a half glass full type of person. Optimists are people who can be in the middle of a hurricane, yet still see some type of silver lining. An optimistic person is able to take the good out of a situation, and they don't waste a good crisis by not seeing opportunity in it. In order to be successful and ascend to your greatness you have to be the optimism in the room full of cynicism and negativity. I can hear the talking points already: Dr. Gray, you don't know what's going on in my life, or Dr. Gray, you don't know how bad this situation is. Trust me, I am not minimizing any issue of circumstance you may be facing, but I can tell you that your response is the key to overcoming them. I want you to know that being optimistic in crisis is not being naïve or gullible. It's called leadership. A good leader remains optimistic because they know that they will find a way to make it happen. They know that their attitude has a direct impact on their outcomes. When I say leader, I really mean being a leader of oneself. You are the chief leader of your life.

What you tell yourself is possible becomes not just possible, but also probable.

Finally, the N in CHAMPIO**N** is for "**N**ever quit mentality." Having a never quit mentality means no matter what the season of your life may be, no matter how many rejections you get, no matter how many ups and downs you go through, you got to have that "quitting is not an option" mentality. I am very familiar with that approach and even wrote a book with the title, "Quitting Was Not an Option," which chronicles a few slices of my life which I believe epitomize the concept of resilience and perseverance. In order to be great, you will have to navigate the rough seas every now and then. You have to, first and foremost, decide that the word quit will not become a part of your lexicon. You may adapt, adjust, reset, pivot, etc. but you have to buy into changing your goals to musts which essentially mean you cannot and will not quit. Champions keep pushing until they find a way. They recognize that time is of the essence. Thinking about time, I am reminded of Michael Phelps who currently holds 28 Olympic medals in swimming; clearly a champion's champion. He conditioned and pushed himself down to the millimeters of seconds. Champions keep punching until the obstacles in their way eventually move. Champions keep pressing on until they eventually reach the finish line. Champions keep moving right along until they have reached their desired destination - and quite honestly, by that time they've upgraded from destination to destiny... they never quit on their hopes, dreams, goals, or their true destiny.

So, what I hope you've seen in this short time you invested with me, is that you are a CHAMPION and that you have what it takes to tap into your **CHAMPION** DNA. With that being said, I want to take a moment to simply remind you what being a champion means. Once you master your champion DNA you will Just Do It and not even blink at the idea that It Takes a Little More to Make a Champion. Let's work together to make you the champion you already are. Reach out to me and I'll show you how to get in touch with your inner CHAMPION. As a token of my appreciation for the time you invested with me, please visit my website at www.DrJohnEGray.com to get your free copy of my E-Book "From Passion to Purpose."

~ About Dr. John E. Gray ~

Dr. John Gray is a Purpose and Resilience Coach who works with people of all ages to empower them to use their God-given purpose, gifts and talents to become the best version of themselves so they can leave a lasting legacy for the Universe.

John strongly believes that we each have a divine purpose in life and that we are much happier and more productive when we are walking in that purpose. He is of the strong conviction that when individuals lead a purpose-driven life; the Kingdom is a much better place for everyone.

Dr. Gray is an accomplished public speaker and protégé of internationally renowned motivational speaker, Les Brown. He is also the host of a weekly talk show, *"PowerTalk."*

Dr. Gray is the Senior Pastor of the Empowered Life Ministries Church in New Jersey. He is also faculty at Stockton University in Galloway, NJ, where he is a professor in the *Ed.D in Organizational Leadership* program.

The Positive Drip and Onyx Expressions Publishing, LLC
Presents
RELENTLESS
EMPOWERING STORIES OF
OVERCOMING ADVERSITY
MY CHAPTER
"FREE TO BE ME"
BRIAR MUNRO
Contributing Author

3: Free To Be Me

By Briar Munro

I am a fixer, a fighter, and oh yeah, a survivor, too, but...

My world was rocked the day I received a phone call from the police informing me that he had been released and that my restraining order had run out. I was nervous. He knew where I worked and where I lived. I was on guard all the time. I literally feared for my life. I never thought I would live past the age of 30.

While I'm happy to still be alive today at 43 years-old, it is with good reason that I doubted I would make it beyond 30 years-old. My survival was a question in my mind many times.

Let's take a quick journey to look at the many things that seemed to be pointing to the possibility that I was going to live a very short life. I was born with a number of physical issues. I had so many surgeries before the age of three that my parents lost count. My childhood was riddled with challenges and setbacks, including both medical issues and learning disabilities. I spent my childhood in and out of doctors' offices and hospitals. I was told over and over again that I was an anomaly and that I was "baffling."

You know what I find *baffling*? I find it really *baffling* that I am still alive. I had many things that made me feel like I was broken, not whole, that I was undeserving of love and attention. That being said, I was blessed with an amazing family. My parents were my first mindset teachers. They taught me how to persevere, how to focus on what I wanted in life, how to set goals, and how to never allow others to place labels on me. I recall one time when my doctors wanted me to be in a wheelchair while waiting for one of my surgeries, and my parents let them know how ridiculous that was. I was an athlete. I had grown up in the dance studio and at age eight, my parents had enrolled me in martial arts to help me develop self-confidence and come out of my shell. I was super quiet and shy.

I was also a people pleaser. I would do anything to ensure that I was liked, and that people felt I was useful. I went out of my way to make sure that they wanted me around. I did my best to help and try to "fix" people; not just in my career, but in my personal life as well. If someone was disappointed in me, I thought it was worse than just about anything.

I think it's that people pleaser mindset that got me in the relationship that nearly cost me my life. I wish I could say that it all happened so quickly, but I really can't. There were definitely signs and red flags along the way that I chose to ignore. I was really trying to make it work.

I think my chief reason for trying so hard was that I felt that I couldn't "get" the good guys. I attracted the men who seemed broken, dependent, and those who needed me. I always felt like I was the only one doing what was needed to keep the relationship going. It didn't even matter if I wasn't happy or knew it was destined for disaster. I still gave it my all to try to make it work.

On the outside, I was a young, fit, confident, ambitious, independent businesswoman who knew exactly what she wanted in life and went out and took it.

On the inside, I felt broken, unworthy, undeserving of happiness, depressed and sad. My underlying feelings about my physical body were impacting the rest of my life.

At this point on my journey, I was living alone in an apartment in Toronto and waiting for my condo to be built that I had purchased all on my own. I was walking down the road and bumped into an old friend; someone I had grown up with at the martial arts studio. Someone I had once had a crush on and felt that he didn't really even know who I was or that I existed, for that matter. He had never given me the time of day back then. He had gone on to become a world class fighter.

We reconnected, chatted once in a while, and then he was arrested for drug possession. He wrote to me from jail and before I knew it, I was brought into his world. I felt sorry for him and believed the story he told me about what he said had happened that resulted in him going to jail. It was clear to me that he needed someone to trust in him and help him get back on his feet.

So, when he was released, I was now part of his world.

We started dating and seeing each other regularly. He had nowhere to live, and I was still waiting for my condo to be built, so we got an apartment together.

Life was good for a while as we settled into a regular routine. I helped him get a job and get on his feet. Soon I would discover that he was a cocaine addict and had been lying about his jail situation.

We began finding him support, counseling, and recovery programs, all while helping him keep his job and me maintaining mine. I was fully entwined.

That's when things took a turn. He began having rage outbursts. Tiny things would set him off. Things so small, I can't even remember what they were. He would scream, throw things, break things to punish me, make everything into my fault and made me second guess every word I said, action I took, and decision I made.

I was being broken down more and more each day and my low self-esteem continued to plummet. I was also withdrawing from my family and friends, as I was ashamed of my situation.

One night, things escalated out of control. His anger took a turn, and he started hitting me. I don't remember how it began, but I ended up being on the floor in the fetal position as he kicked me over and over. My shins, my forearms, elbows, ribs, and head were hit over and over again and I remember thinking, "This is it. I am going to die here on the floor of my bedroom. This is the night it's all going to end."

I don't know what made him stop, but the next thing I remember is he was holding me tightly and rationalizing what he had done. He brushed it off as if it was nothing. I couldn't leave. He was "hugging me" and I felt that if I tried to get up and go, he would start again. Even though I was afraid, I told him I was fine and downplayed the whole incident as if I agreed with him that it was no big deal.

The next morning, when I awoke, he was gone. I packed a bag and got in the car. I went to work and then headed to my parents to tell them what had happened. But once I got there, I couldn't bring myself to tell them. I ended up telling lies about why I was there. I explained my bruises and soreness by telling them I had fallen in my bathroom.

I was embarrassed and couldn't believe I had let myself get into this situation. I was ashamed and didn't know how they would react. I let my negative self-talk take over and told myself that I deserved this. I convinced myself that I was going to die soon anyway, so what was the point in going through the hurt and anguish that was to come if I told anyone what was really going on with me. I felt it was my own fault, and that I had to live with the decisions I had made. This was pretty much how I had always been.

I'll digress for a moment so you can understand me a little more. As I grew up, I decided that I was put on this earth to help people. I believe that I was given all my struggles so that I could be empathic and relate to others to help them along their journey and to overcome adversity.

I still believe this. In fact, I went to college and became a personal trainer and health coach. I spent my early adulthood working with clients to live their best, healthiest, and happiest life. I created my own company, and opened a studio, which helped hundreds of people turn their lives around.

My office was at a children's dance studio. I continued to work through the days, helping others become healthy and happy and I would return home each night miserable. I felt like a fraud and an imposter. I knew I was good at my job, but underneath, I believed I was undeserving of my success.

Well, back to boyfriend... I didn't completely break it off with him, but he sensed I was distancing myself from him and he was worried about me leaving him. He turned up the controlling behavior. Then one day, he was calling and texting me non-stop. The messages came by the 10's and 20's on a daily basis, but this day was different.

He started to threaten me in the messages and said that if I didn't answer him, he would come find me. I was afraid he would show up at the studio when the kids were around. So, I decided it was time to take action. I didn't tell my family, but I did go to the police. I spent the entire day there as I told them my story, spoke about why I hadn't left, took recordings of the voicemail and text messages. They explained to me what his rap sheet actually looked like. There were years and years of things in his police file that he hadn't told me about. I was stunned.

That was the day I realized that it wasn't my fault. That was the start of my rebuilding. I finally concluded I had been manipulated, strung along, and used. It was apparent that he was taking advantage of my good nature and willingness to help him.

Eventually, I learned just how strong I was inside and out. I took the hard step of telling my parents about my situation. I moved out of the apartment and began working through my emotions. I got a restraining order, and he was arrested, yet again. I had to go to court with a lawyer who spoke on my behalf and he was sent back to jail. I moved on with my life.

After this, I began to really work on myself again. I was healthy physically, but I needed to do the mental work. I focused on myself and learned the power we have to change our world by changing our thoughts. I was determined to change my mindset and actually became certified as a mindset coach. Mindset is more than just being positive or counting our blessings. Do those things help? Yes, of course they do, but that won't change everything. We need to understand our brain and how it works. When we understand why we are the way we are and why we make the decisions we make, we can make better choices.

I learned to listen to my gut. Intuition is so very strong and can play a huge role in our lives if we trust it. Women, especially, seem to have this gift. It takes practice and patience with ourselves to get into the habit of listening to our intuition, but it is powerful.

I learned that I cannot help everyone. I figured out that I am not the designated "fixer." Ultimately, I concluded that we cannot help those who don't want to be helped. I also came to terms with the fact that it's not my job to help everyone. I get to choose who I help and it cannot come at a cost to my own health and wellbeing. Again, this took time to learn and settle into a new version of myself, but it was possible.

Then, I began rebuilding my self-esteem and self-worth. This part took a lot longer. It meant surrounding myself with people who love me and finding friends and relationships with people who treat me with respect and support. I began to believe that I am valuable, worthy, and needed in this world.

Fast forward to the new version of myself; now, as a mother of two boys, I have another job. My priority is to raise independent, kind, loving, and giving humans who will impact the world in a positive way. I want to model the importance of being empathetic human beings who understand how to treat others. I teach them that everyone around them has feelings that are important and they should respect them.

Lastly, I am reminded that I am a survivor. I am still here on this earth and I am here for a reason. I still believe that I have gone through everything that I have so that I can better understand, empathize, and help others with compassion and understanding. I took the steps to get out of that horrible situation, move forward, and become whole again. My hope is that my story can empower others who find themselves trapped in toxic, unhealthy situations that threaten their wellbeing to be willing to do the necessary *heart work*. I hope that through my story, others can see the power that our mindsets have in determining the type of life we live.

If you are reading this and can relate, I want to remind you of something incredibly important…

YOU are valuable. YOU are needed on this earth. YOU are loved and deserve to be happy, safe, and healthy.

If you need guidance and support and want to believe in believing again, please reach out to me. I'm here and ready to help you to proudly embrace your internal spirit, which screams, "I'm free to be me."

www.briarmunro.com

~ About Briar Munro ~

As a child, Briar was diagnosed with Perthes disease, a degeneration of the bones, in her hip. Despite living with ongoing pain and repeated surgeries, Briar continued to train as a dancer and martial artist. She learned early on the importance of creating healthy, balanced practices for her mind and body in order to have the lifestyle that she wanted. After completing her *Personal Trainer and Lifestyle Coach Certificate*, Briar began coaching her clients to do the same. Since then, she has worked with hundreds of clients and helped them level up and balance life, family, and business while finding solutions to their health and wellness struggles.

Briar began working as a personal trainer in 2001, but wanted to create a better environment for her clients to reach their goals. In 2006, she opened *Fly Girl Fitness*, one of the top private gyms in the east Toronto area. Combining traditional personal training with her Pilates, dance, martial arts, and mindset coaching backgrounds, Briar created programs that were unique and effective for her clients in a space that was comfortable and invigorating. Since closing her physical doors, Briar has worked virtually with clients from around the world to create that same atmosphere of positivity, safety, and encouragement.

Living with Perthes disease, Briar knows that healthy exercise, nutrition, and mindset is the difference between life in a wheelchair and life hiking through the woods with her two young children. These are the principles that inform her work with clients so they can be their best selves.

Find her on Instagram @briarmunro12 and through her website @ www.briarmunro.com

The Positive Drip and Onyx Expressions Publishing, LLC

Presents

RELENTLESS

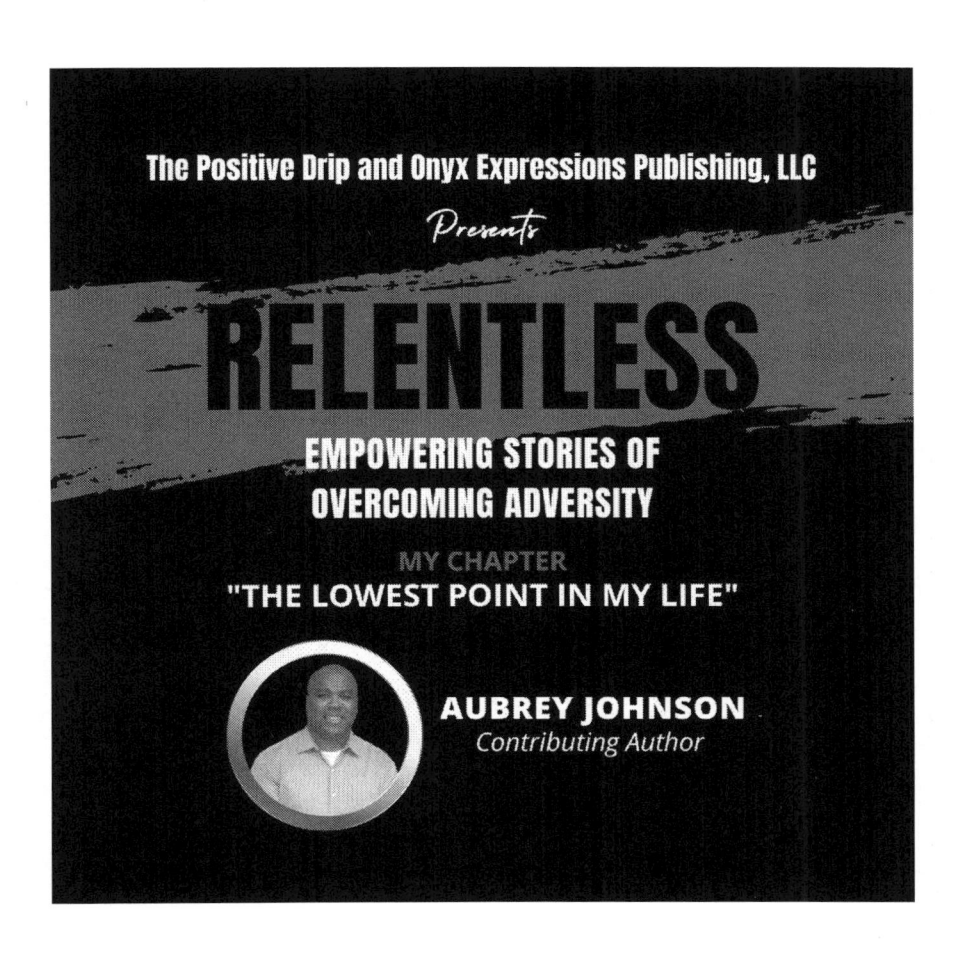

EMPOWERING STORIES OF OVERCOMING ADVERSITY

MY CHAPTER
"THE LOWEST POINT IN MY LIFE"

AUBREY JOHNSON
Contributing Author

4: The Lowest Point in my Life

By Aubrey Johnson

Wow, I just met "the one." I can't explain it, but deep down inside I know she is "the one." I haven't even dated her for three months, but I already know... she's "the one." I can't believe these words are swimming around in my head - and my heart. This makes no sense to me, my mantra is "Work Hard, Play Hard." It's the summer of 1996, I'm 28 years old, single and don't have any children. I'm enjoying life. I just got a promotion at work and my reward to myself is a laser-red Ford Mustang... Yes, life is good. My plan is to squeeze every essence possible out of it.

I worked hard, putting in the effort and long hours, so felt I deserved to play hard. In my mind, I was justified in playing as hard as I could. You may be wondering what does my "play hard" consist of? At that time in my life, playing hard meant all-night parties, nightclubs, weekend getaways, and more.

One night, midway through that summer while out playing hard, I met "the one" at a dance club. Of course, I didn't know it that night, but I would quickly come to realize she was "the one." Her name was Sherry. The funny thing is I had dated her previously, about five years before, so this was actually a re-acquaintance. We got re-acquainted, exchanged numbers, and started dating again. Something was different this time, though. Little did I know my life was about to be TOTALLY changed.

Sherry was a single mother, a homeowner, and had a great career as a Teacher. She was beyond the "wild and crazy" lifestyle – after all, she was raising her daughter. Dating Sherry caused me to "tone down" my usual level of intense partying and drinking. Even though it was toned down, I could see it was still a little bit too much for her. She had a lot of responsibility at home and at work. So I wanted to give her a "break" from her usual home life and parenting, even if for just a short time, to get away and have some fun. We went out a few more times. It seemed all good for a moment, but despite my toned-down partying, it was still too intense and wild for Sherry. Simply put, she was at a different point in her life. Her priorities were different. She had responsibilities as a homeowner, Teacher, and mother. After just three months of dating, Sherry broke up with me. This stung! It really hurt!!

My response to the breakup was confusing to me. I felt isolated. As much as I knew she was "the one," I didn't feel I could talk to anyone about it because of the short time we dated. I mean, how do you know that she's "the one" after just 3 short months? It reminded me of a song that was released around that time called "Nobody Knows" by the Tony Rich

Project – specifically the lyrics "...and I'm crying inside, and nobody knows it but me."

I couldn't stop thinking about her. Sitting alone in my apartment was too much to bear, so I would escape, and hit the bars and nightclubs. I realized that Sherry was "the one" that got away. I missed her and it hurt. Anything I could do to avoid and cover my sadness and broken heart, I would do. This resulted in me ratcheting up my partying – going out to a different bar every night, including weeknights, meeting women I wasn't interested in, but who catered to my ego. I was spending money like crazy. I'm sure you can see where this is going. Just about all of my money was going to the bars, as I horribly slipped behind on my telephone bill, car note, and rent.

Shortly after the breakup, one October evening, a buddy and I went out to one of our usual nightspots. We met two young ladies. It wasn't long before the drinks were flowing, with lots of dancing, joking, and laughing. After the nightclub, they invited us to their apartment and kept the fun going. By now it was 3:00 a.m., early Wednesday morning, and I had to be at work at 8:00 a.m. My buddy and I left their apartment at 4:30am, and made the 45-minute drive back to my apartment (how we made it back with as much as we drank, I don't know...). Anyhow, my buddy leaves, and I set my alarm for 7:30am and hit the pillow.

My eyes open, and I check the clock: it's 11:30 a.m.! I crawl out of bed and take myself to the bathroom for that hard look in the mirror. Staring back at me was a familiar sight: Red eyes - check. Exhausted face - check. Inescapable smell of alcohol on my breath and pores - check. I was used to all that. BUT, I also noticed these nasty looking splotches all over my neck! I don't know how they got there – I had too much to drink to remember!! I've gone into work hung over and smelling of alcohol masked with peppermint many times before, and I could have gone into work this day; but the splotches were much too noticeable - I couldn't hide them, nor explain how they got there. So, I did something I've always prided myself on NEVER doing – I called in sick. That was my first moment of shame that day. I walked outside to my car to make sure I didn't damage it during my blacked out driving home earlier that morning. Coming back to my door, there's a note from my apartment complex – a notice that my rent is late - 2 months late. I have a pounding headache, *cotton mouth*, shaky hands, and splotches all over my neck. I can't think of anything to do but sit down in my living room. I feel paralyzed.

As I'm sitting there, alone and feeling ashamed of myself, my telephone rings. It's the bank that financed my car. I'm now three months behind in my payments. They tell me I need to send a payment of at least $600 in less than 48 hours, or they'll come pick up the car. Three months? Really? Now, I'm really feeling paralyzed. I don't know what to do. I can't keep ignoring knocks on the door and phone calls. I'm still just sitting there, wallowing in my despair and wondering what I was going to do to get out of this mess. After 4 hours of staring at the wall, I noticed no one was calling. I decided to call my buddy to make sure he made it home safely. So, I dialed his number and there it was: the dreaded recorded message telling me my service was interrupted for non-payment (you have to remember this was before cell phones were common). This is definitely the lowest point of my life.

Wow, this is crazy! What do I do now? How do I get $600 within 48 hours to keep my car? How do I get caught up with my rent to avoid being tossed in the street? I can truly tell you that I've NEVER felt more alone in my life than I did that day. I can't even make a phone call if I want to; I phone service is shut off. I looked out the window – it's overcast, foggy, and drizzling rain. Then it hit me: something I didn't want to do, but knew I had to do. Ever since grade school, I played the saxophone in the band, including middle and high school. I was pretty good at the time. This saxophone was the one item I had in my life that I treasured, and proud to say was mine. I was proud of my history with it, and all that I accomplished with it. As a confused, nervous kid growing up, it was my first empowering source of confidence. So, after a lot of thought, I reluctantly put my saxophone in my car, and drove in the foggy, cold rain to a very rough side of town to pawn it. They only offered me $50, but in my desperation, I accepted it. As I drove back home, I continued trying to figure out where I was going to get the rest of the money I needed.

I made the "long walk of shame" from the parking lot to my apartment door. I can't describe the nervousness and anxiety I felt while walking to my door. I was hoping not to see another notice hung on the doorknob, or worse, a dead-lock on it. Thankfully, there wasn't, so I walked in, sat down on my couch, and continued staring at the wall. I don't know what to do or where to turn. Then all of a sudden, while staring at the wall, I think about Sherry, and I start to cry. All this time, I ran to avoid thinking about her; but there was no running now. I had nowhere to go. I was alone AND lonely. I was at my lowest point. I had to face the pain that I should have faced and processed shortly after she broke up with me months ago. So, that's what I did at that moment. I realized that life must go on. She moved on. I didn't have to like it, but I realized I had to move on. I had to LEARN how to be alone, and make more mature, responsible decisions to get myself out of this rut!

Long story, short...I did just that. I got through that uncomfortable moment. It was definitely difficult, but somehow I moved forward. Fast forward to March of 2001... In the near 5 years since my crisis, a lot changed, and a lot stayed the same. I married, became a father, and divorced, so I was single again. Clearly, a lot has happened since the crisis; some good and some bad. By this time, I was living in a spare bedroom with my parents until the divorce was finalized. My "work hard, play hard" mantra is far behind me at this point. I rarely went out anymore, but one evening as I was trying to put myself together again, I decided to clear my head and go to the neighborhood pub for a drink. Funny how the Universe works; I ran into a familiar face. I'm sure you can guess who I ran into? That's right – Sherry! I mean, what are the chances??? We sit down and catch up about what's happened over the past 5 years. Turns out she was married and divorced at that time too! She is at a different place in her life, and I'm at a different place in mine. Throughout the rest of 2001, we grow closer and start to see each other again. We became engaged in August of 2005, and married in July 2006.

Think about that. She breaks up with me in 1996, and we marry in 2006. After that sad phone call that Saturday morning in October 1996, if you would have told me I would marry that woman 10 years later, I would have not only disagreed, but would have called you crazy.

But wait, there's more! At some point in our marriage, I couldn't help but break down to Sherry, now my wife, and tell her about that lowest point in my life that I just shared with you. I told her that I had pawned my saxophone and never got it back.

Unbeknownst to me, soon after, she tells me she has a surprise. That surprise turned out to be a new saxophone! I'm middle-aged now, and it's been years since I've played that instrument on a regular basis, but I was blessed by God and the Universe in such an amazing way with Sherry. My saxophone was evidence of the coming of the full circle of my life. Guess what, Sherry was and is "the one!!" Once I worked on myself and did what

I had to do to get myself together, I got my lady back AND my saxophone!

I have learned a TREMENDOUS amount of lessons from this journey. Lessons of humility. Lessons of processing. Lessons of hurt and pain. Lessons of accountability and maturity. I can truly say I would have NEVER learned these lessons if I never had the struggles. I have overcome!

I'm happy to report, we now have four grandchildren, live in Texas, and have been happily married for 16 years and counting! I shared all this with you to let you know that there is always hope. You may not get it right in the beginning, but if you stay the course and keep the faith, you can have what you buried years before. I say that to say that everything that's buried may not actually be buried, it may be planted instead. So, plant the seeds of your desire and nurture them... Eventually, harvest time will come, in due season. The struggle is real, but the rewards are really good! Your lowest point just may lead you to your highest point.

~ About Aubrey Johnson ~

Aubrey Johnson is the Creator and Host of *The Road to Rediscovery Podcast*. Aubrey is originally from Cincinnati, Ohio, and currently lives in North Dallas, Texas.

Aubrey believes every person has a story to tell. Some stories serve to entertain, others to teach. He first conceptualized *The Road to Rediscovery* to provide a platform for these ordinary, yet extraordinary, people to share their stories in the hopes of helping others who may be suffering through dark times of their own.

The Road to Rediscovery podcast invites listeners to travel along on the journey of life. Through the words of each week's guests, listeners have the chance to reflect upon their own lives and perhaps, find lessons they can learn from throughout.

Aubrey's guests share stories of overcoming great odds to transform their lives. How did they make it through? How did those moments go on to shape their later years?

Aubrey feels it's an honor to be alongside his guests as they tap into incredible wells of inner strength to share their stories with others. These stories are sometimes raw and always real. The question is, will we ignore these life lessons and move on, or rediscover them, and grow?

Above all, Aubrey wants his listeners and guests to know they're not alone. By walking this road together, we are all stronger.

Aubrey sums it all up by saying, *"A unique thing about the show is how it's both introspective and retrospective, which is part of its beauty. Be it guest interviews or solo episodes, they each lend themselves to a deep observance within for awareness of self and reflection with the purpose of learning and growth."*

Download/Subscribe: You can subscribe to The Road to Rediscovery and listen to all episodes online at www.road2rediscovery.com, on Apple Podcasts, or wherever you listen to your shows (Spreaker, Spotify, etc.)

The Positive Drip and Onyx Expressions Publishing, LLC
Presents
RELENTLESS
EMPOWERING STORIES OF
OVERCOMING ADVERSITY
MY CHAPTER
"THIS CANDY IS GOOD FOR YOU"
LY SMITH
Contributing Author

5:
This CANDY is Good For You

By Ly Smith

I am not one to be superstitious, but I do find it entertaining to consider that my birth date falls within the Leo sun sign in astrology. The lion is a representation of Leo, which is a large cat. You may have heard of the old myth or wives' tale that cats have nine lives. Looking at my own "cat-like self" I would say that I have lived about seven of those lives.

Les Brown, my mentor with the Power Voice Academy during the 2020 pandemic, likes to say, "When life takes you down, be sure to fall on your back. Because if you can look up, you can get up!"

Would it be valuable if I shared just one of my seven lives and why I am so incredibly excited about life today?

6:57 PM, 30 December, 2016

I was watching the tangerine sun set upon the sapphire blue horizon of the Pacific Ocean. My husband was just a few steps away toward my right, with his camera lens extended from his nose like Pinocchio, moving back and forth, twisting the lens in his hand to get the perfect light and angle.

My girl was also to my right, cradled in my arm as we shared a tender mother-daughter moment. On my left, my stepson and his girlfriend were cuddling in the golden light.

In my mind, I was thinking how grateful I was to be blessed with a 23-day vacation across these four islands of paradise, sharing a grand holiday and all these amazing sunsets with my family.

I thought to myself, "I am having an experience not everyone gets even once in a lifetime."

And then I observed that I was having only a thought.

Why?

Why was I not feeling this moment? What was happening? Who was I standing on this shore with the breeze caressing my hair?

In high school, I was known as "Living Loving Laughing Ly" because I lived life to its fullest with no apology, no holding back.

And yet, this time...I found myself being suffocated by "*just*." Yes, that is dust with a "j." I realized I was covered in metaphorical specks of *just* a wife, *just* a stay-at-home mom, *just* a stepmom, *just* a daughter, *just* a sister...

I was *just* a woman, standing on the beach as an empty shell of a human being.

My thoughts brought to my attention and awareness that I was depressed and had been for some time.

While I pondered how long I had been in this state, I decided to focus on my truth that "enough was enough" and I no longer wanted to feel this way.

Next, a question entered my thought space, "Ly, what *does* make you happy?"

I knew what would make my husband happy. We had been married for fifteen years, though the present days were not particularly happy ones. I knew what would appease my stepson, though he was already out on his own. Unfortunately, we did not have the best of relationships. I knew what would bring a smile to my teenage daughter's face even though we were in that tough phase of adolescence.

But as for me? I was clueless. With the New Year only days away, the one thing I knew for sure was that I was going to make it a priority to go on a quest to move from *clueless* to *clarity*.

As I continued to stand there pondering, I realized I wanted a word to support my journey. I had heard of friends choosing a word for the year, but it was not a practice I had implemented before.

The word "laugh" came to mind, and I thought it was perfect, especially since I could not remember when was the last time I had a real heart-felt laugh. I believed if I could get reacquainted with laughter, this would anchor my quest and help me get through the edge of the depression so I could get to the other side.

When I returned stateside, I chose to do anything and everything that would make me laugh. I went on a mission to laugh.

My journey began with hanging out on the corner of the couch, watching reruns of "Friends", my favorite sitcom. Admittedly, no matter how many times I watched the shows, knowing most of the lines and what's coming next, I would still laugh.

I was very fortunate during this time that a very talented local comedy troupe put on weekly improv shows. So, nearly every weekend, I made it my business to be at the theater, front and center, getting my laugh on, working out my sides and working out my cheeks.

I was active within my local community, partaking in networking opportunities, making connections, and building relationships. I knew the people who had an amazing sense of humor, so I figured if I could get in their space, their humor and positivity would rub off on me energetically.

AFTER SEVERAL MONTHS, AN INCREDIBLE THING HAPPENED.

I felt something like a golden light break through what seemed like dark mud caked over my heart. As the darkness crumbled away, the light seemed to ooze up my side and crawl into my left ear, whispering, "Now that I'm here, what would you like to do with me?"

Behind the question, I heard a little girl laughing with such delight.

I thought, "This must be JOY!"

And I recognized the little girl as my eight-year-old self as she asked me, "Remember that feeling? Let's go chasing that again!"

When I was 8 years old, I was a very confident reader. I enjoyed reading aloud at school and in my catechism classes. My catechist teacher asked me if I would proclaim the scriptures at an upcoming mass. I emphatically responded, "Yes!"

I remember approaching the ambo, reading the holy words, and seeing smiles across the 300 family members in the congregation.

I was not fazed by all the faces staring back at me. I didn't know what it was to have stage fright. Those thoughts and words were not part of my vocabulary or my experience.

And the real magic happened when I exited the sanctuary. A bit of a shiver ran through my tiny body, and I thought, "What is this feeling? How do I get more of it?"

My greatest dreams were to be a public speaker and to be a stay-at-home mom. I *stuck a pin* in my first dream, which I now know is my calling to become a corporate motivational speaker. Instead, I focused on my other dream: to be a stay-at-home mom.

I lived out that dream for many years before it became clear to me that my other dream continued to hang in the balance. I had forgotten about the pin until it became obvious to me that NOW was the time to pull it out and begin to dream again! It was my time to integrate my personal development studies from the previous twenty-five years and my personal stories from the past forty-ish years into speaking and to begin creating impact and making a difference in the world.

It had only been a few years before since I had slowly descended into a down spiral of massive depression. For a long time, I didn't even notice what was happening. Then I started paying attention to how lacklustre my general day-to-day affect had become. Now that I was aware of it, I realized I had to do something about it. I braved the necessary baby steps to climb my way back up to who I originally wanted to become.

I dug deep into myself, working on my health and vitality because I knew I needed lots of energy to do all the things I wanted to do. I dialed in; paying full attention to how I ate, hydrated, moved, and slept.

I worked on how I showed up in my marriage, which was in figurative *hospice*, waiting for me to either pull the plug or choose life. I took a proverbial hammer to the wall I had built and allowed myself to be vulnerable once again, sharing with my husband the tough conversations around my entrepreneurial ventures and how we needed to communicate so that we could prevent resentment from compounding.

I set monumental goals for myself and took massive action.

I joined Toastmasters International, and four months later, entered a speaking contest. I advanced several times, losing only one step short of going to Nationals.

I sought and achieved several certifications, including Brendon Burchard's High Performance Masters Program, Tony Robbins and Dean Graziosi's Knowledge Broker Blueprint, Dale Carnegie's Skills for Success, and MAPPS.

I disciplined myself with an evening and morning routine so that I could be productive, since I had so much to learn and implement as quickly as possible. I acknowledged my strengths and weaknesses in my personality and habits and used them to grow and evolve into the person I am today.

I learned that I had a zone of genius, my passion for the growth mindset and positive self-talk. I had a gift for speaking, able to articulate a powerful and influential message that would move an audience to action. And I was reminded by Les Brown that I have greatness within me.

Today, I am living the dream of my eight-year-old self. I continually say, "Yes!" to my calling to show up and serve others in a mighty way, whether it's on stage, on camera, or in meetings.

I guide entrepreneurs and coaches who want to use speaking to grow their business, but struggle to recognize their amazingness and teach them how to stand in their power so that they can shine with dynamic presence, certainty, and confidence.

WHAT HAVE I LEARNED THAT I WANT TO SHARE WITH YOU?

When I went on my quest to explore what makes me happy, I learned that not many people really know what makes them happy. Going from clueless to clarity sparked my journey.

When I chose the word "laugh" to carry me through my journey, I explored and researched the power of self-talk. We have the power to choose our words and the stories we tell ourselves. This alone can make all the difference for how we show up in our lives and how we shape our reality.

When we can begin with the desired end in mind, we can design a roadmap that shows us how to get what we want. When we make the time for each step and schedule those steps in our daily and weekly calendars, we accomplish our goals better and faster.

When we commit to an evening and morning routine or amplify our best habits that serve us, we get out of our own way and continuously and consistently move forward.

When we recognize and own that we have genius, gifts, and greatness to give the world, we find that we easily stand with confidence as we climb toward the next levels of ourselves.

These pieces of learnings have become the heart of my signature coaching process I fondly call the *CANDY* Method: **C**larity ~ **A**ffirmation ~ **N**ecessity ~ **D**iscipline ~ **Y**ou!

I have often heard that speakers typically take their mess and turn it into their message, and they take their traumas and turn them into triumphs. What we've been through can provide seeds of hope for others and teach them how to get to the other side where they can live or experience their best lives.

In sharing my story with you, I am on a mission to transform the REACTORS into CREATORS.

The REACTORS are the persons who live by circumstance and convenience, believing that life is happening *to* them. They feel stuck in the day-to-day of life as they put out fire after fire and whatever distraction, interruption, or expectation comes at them. They think they are goal setters, but they never really accomplish them because they are so caught up in the moment. They often go to bed exhausted and wonder, "Do I really get to wake up tomorrow and do it all over again?!"

The CREATORS are the persons who live by clarity and commitment. They believe that life happens *for* them. They know they can't control everything, but they can control their thoughts and how they respond to whatever distraction, interruption, or expectation comes at them. They see themselves first, so they can clearly see what matters most to them. They set their goals and get productive by striving toward those goals. They often go to bed satisfied and wonder, "Do I really get to wake up tomorrow and do it all over again?!"

When you look closely at the words REACTORS and CREATORS, you will see they are anagrams, meaning they are words with the exact same letters, just in a different order. The fun part is that the difference between these two words is in how you see "C" yourself! Do you see yourself as a creator or as a reactor?

Be RELENTLESS in pursuit of your happiness and share your story with others.

YOU MATTER, YOUR MESSAGE MATTERS, AND THE AUDIENCE WHO NEEDS TO HEAR YOUR STORY MATTERS! LET ME OFFER YOU SOME C.A.N.D.Y.

~ About Ly Smith ~

Ly Smith is the Speaker and Presentations Consultant with UpCycle Coaching, who guides entrepreneurs to own their stage with dynamic presence, certainty, and confidence. She is the creator of The CANDY Method for Speaking Confidently and show host of "UpCycle Your Life" on WIN-WIN Women TV.

Ly is a three-time bestselling author, an award-winning international speaker, certified life coach, and a certified NLP Master Practitioner and Time Line Therapy Practitioner.

In addition to her passion for speaking and high-performance, Ly is a wife and mother of two amazing kiddos. She loves coffee, cooking, and getting outdoors for walks, hikes, and snowshoeing.

Ly is driven to help entrepreneurs to see the best within themselves and to accept: NO EXCUSES, ONLY EXCELLENCE!

The Positive Drip and Onyx Expressions Publishing, LLC
Presents

RELENTLESS

EMPOWERING STORIES OF OVERCOMING ADVERSITY

MY CHAPTER
"THE DIFFERENCE IN THINKING"

KARL DAVIDSON
Contributing Author

6:
The Difference in Thinking

by Karl Davidson

My adversity was one of an internal battle I had to overcome when I learned about financial education and entrepreneurship at the ripe old age of 25. I was never taught that growing up. I wasn't taught it in school or college. You see, I did what society and my parents taught me to do. I had the good grades, I had a degree in electrical engineering. I had the steady paycheck job. But, what I wasn't programmed in was entrepreneurship, time, and financial freedom. I had not been shown the other side of the coin or the difference in thinking. Unlearning what I learned and relearning a totally different mindset on a daily basis. One that flicks back and forth due to fears, insecurities, and the old question of "what will people think?" I am going to explain to you three different set of core principles that will help you overcome adversity and that have streamlined my journey of entrepreneurship. Applying these three principles – Time, Energy and Work - over the past seven years has made me the entrepreneur I am today.

TIME

Time is the first one. We all have time. But time is like a double-edged sword. It is slowly killing you. As you read this, you are probably closer to your death than you are your birth. Let that sink in. Time is really your most valuable asset. Yes, we will touch on some financial education in this chapter as well. I know from working with many people; they love to make money and in doing so help more people. So how do you value your time? What is it you do with it? Do you go to your job Monday to Friday, 9-5 and then come home, grab dinner, and if you have kids play with the kids? If you're in a relationship maybe you go to a restaurant (of course, not every night!) or maybe you go to the cinema? Maybe you go to the gym and work out? Maybe you play football, tennis, or MMA. Maybe you play some video games on the PlayStation or Xbox (which one is better? 😊) Or do you scroll endlessly watching people fight on Facebook or funny cat or dog videos? So, what do you do? Write it out on a piece of paper. Write down what your typical day looks like, including if you are in a job. Becoming aware of where you are losing time is going to be a game-changer on your journey into entrepreneurship. I equate time with discipline. Especially when you want to be an entrepreneur. Entrepreneurs are disciplined people. I find some people are very punctual, while others, not so much. Some have their systems in place, others not so much. Some people love writing lists, others try and remember everything in their head. So, plan out your day and stick to it like industrial strength glue!

Once you know what it is you do throughout the day, write it on paper and be detailed! The more detail, the better. This will help you become aware of what exactly you can sacrifice (not forever, just for a short time) in order to pursue your entrepreneurship journey and achieve your goals. One big thing that I sacrificed was going to watch my beloved Arsenal football team on weekdays and weekends, but I knew if I sacrificed watching them now, down the road I would be watching them from a corporate box at the stadium or in the stands with the crowd. Another one was giving up alcohol. It didn't serve me and I didn't see any value in going to the pub; it just cost me a lot of money! So, getting back to time and discipline... How disciplined are you when it comes to time and time management? Personally, I don't believe in time management. What I believe in is priority management. Remember those lists of things you have to do, well, all you have to do is organize these into boxes! See The Eisenhower Matrix below for an example of a priority matrix that you can use:

	Urgent	**Not Urgent**
Important	DO IT NOW	PLAN IT Schedule a time to do it
Not Important	DELEGATE IT Who can do it for you?	DROP IT Eliminate it

Unfortunately, you will have to drop some things to pick up better things. Better skills. Better information. Think of this as two marshmallows *later* instead of one *now*. It's the growth mindset rather than the fixed mindset. Your future self will thank you for it. Trust me on that. Dropping certain activities or hobbies is needed for becoming an entrepreneur. Know where you are leaking time and then follow the matrix in the figure above to clean up and reorganize what it is you must do on a daily basis to reach your goals.

ENERGY

Energy and the amount of it you have will determine how much you can achieve in your whole life span. Ever found yourself low in energy? That's ok! It happens. The main thing is that if it's constant low energy, something has to change. As Jim Rohn says, "You are not a tree, you can move." But what happens when you don't want to move? Sure, it's okay to have a rest day. You just have to learn when to rest. Just don't quit on yourself or your vision. There will be times when you are in low energy mode, but just remember WHY you started doing whatever it is you are doing in the first place. In 2017, I went to a retreat in Bali, hosted by a beautiful couple. One of hosts said to the attendees, "What's the number one rule when you are on a rollercoaster?". I'm sure we all thought to ourselves, "I don't know, maybe wear your seatbelt!" But what she said to us back then has stuck with me ever since. "NEVER get off when you are upside down!" Your energy might be low, but don't stop. Don't quit. Keep going. Let's get scientific! Here comes a physics law I studied in school and college. Energy is everything. Let me repeat... **Energy is everything.** Isaacs Newton's third law is: For every action, there is an equal and opposite reaction. It's one of my favorite laws, along with the law of attraction. I wasn't aware of the law of attraction until I was 25.

Well, I actually knew about it. I just didn't know that it was called the *law of attraction*. What you focus on expands. What you think you attract.

As a matter of fact, my entire life has been spent trying to help underdogs. This is hard because some people just want to be average. Mediocrity takes lots of victims every day. Most of the time, an underdog doesn't want to be top dog. They are more comfortable being the bottom bitch. Let's talk about food for energy! Disclaimer: Always seek nutritional advice from a professional nutritionist. Do you love food? I do! What do you put in your body? Write down your daily food intake for a week and you'll see exactly what you eat. There are many apps for this if you want to do it on an app. What type of foods and liquids are you putting into your body? Are they good or bad? How's your alcohol intake? Do you smoke? Your body is the only body that you have, so do you treat it like a temple? Obviously, we are human and we all have days where we want that extra piece of cake or decide to get a take away. I encourage you to be super mindful of the food you put in your body. What you put in is what you get out on an energy level. I won't mention any particular diets you should be on, but I have noticed since I turned vegetarian and inching my way towards being vegan, my energy levels have increased and also my conscience is at ease. I do miss eating meat though! Do what feels good for you. As I said before, be super mindful of what you put in your body. If you are feeling lethargic, try changing your diet and see how you feel. Give yourself time though. Remember, we don't do overnight success. Overnight success usually takes ten years. Now, what about your exercise? Disclaimer again - take professional advice from a trained fitness instructor. How often do you exercise? Here's a tip, if you are struggling to consume information, download the Audible app and listen to books while you exercise. You are catching two apples with the one hand! Partake of a 30-minute motivation video or personal development book while doing some weights or cardio will help you so much to increase your energy levels.

Another thing I've noticed is that environment is key when overcoming any adversity and becoming relentless in life. For me, I have always found that different networking events, seminars, and webinars have helped me grow so much. Being around like-minded people on similar paths, experiencing similar issues, makes me feel like I am not alone on my journey. Wow, I remember the very first big event I went to. Let me set the scene for you. There were approx. 4-5000 people in an arena in Rome, Italy. The place was pumping with music. People from all over the world were there. In fact, I even begin to count how many nationalities were represented there. It was amazing! The speakers were highly motivational and motivated me to take action in all aspects of my life! I had been listening to a lot of Eric Thomas and Les Brown audios for a few years on YouTube. I had one of those *enough is enough* moments. Have you ever had them? I looked at myself in the mirror one day and I said, "Damn, Karl. You need to get fit. You need to beef up and tone up." So, I joined a local gym and once I got there, I needed some music to get me going. I typed into YouTube motivation because I figured people in the gym are motivated, right? Eric Thomas came up. The rest is history, as they say. Going through that door led me to big events all across the world. Networking with people from all across the world and learning from different cultures has been very inspirational for me. I would encourage you to take some time and go to events, seminars, and webinars. You just never know who you might meet and what sort of connections you may make or the stories you will hear that may motivate and inspire you to enhance your life. Live a little and *let your hair down,* as they say. It's hard to explain what you learn at big personal development events, but I can tell you it has really been worth it for me. There can be so much content, but fear not, your brain is a muscle, so it will expand as you take in all the new, juicy content and context. This is where big ideas come from. This is where your imagination runs wild and you begin to think of different systems, techniques, and methods for you to expand your business and yourself. You don't always need to go to the Tony Robbins style events. Maybe some smaller events may suit you better. But, I do encourage you to go and try them out... large or small, just go!

Work

Now let's talk about work! Work really, really hard at working really smart!

So, would you rather 100% of your efforts or 1% of 100 people's efforts? I am briefly going to share some financial education here. Entrepreneurs need financial education. Remember, there are three types of education. Financial, professional, and the one that most people know, academic. We have seen that a lot of college "dropouts" become big time CEOs of companies. For example, like that college dropout, Mark Zuckerberg (we all know what he started). A lot of entrepreneurs don't have much academic education. They don't fit into the mold of college. For some entrepreneurs, they wouldn't be where they are if it wasn't for academic education. Knowledge and experience should be the lifelong learning we focus on, as opposed to just formal education. Most people don't invest a cent into their education once they finish formal education and the schooling system. But, when you become an entrepreneur, you NEED to know about money, wealth generation, and business. Now, back to financial education... Entrepreneurs really need to work really, really hard at working really, really smart. Most people just work really, really hard and don't know about working smart. There are always a few that don't work or are just lazy. That's not you though, so let's not waste valuable time and energy focusing on those people. Being a successful entrepreneur requires you to have systems in place. It's what all big companies have. Why be a small one when you can be a big one? It's totally doable... you just need time, effort, a good team and smart work. Oh, yeah... Good habits, too! There are three types of income: earned, portfolio, and passive income. The main difference between an entrepreneur and your average employee is that entrepreneurs will sometimes work for free and the end goal is portfolio and passive income. Work for free, you say? Yes! The attitude comes before the BIG paycheck. Earned income is when you trade your time for money, i.e. a job. You clock in and you clock out and you get your paycheck at the end of the pay period. An entrepreneur works for portfolio and passive income, i.e. they do something once and get paid for it over and over and over. Like a singer, or an insurance salesman or a network marketing representative, they create or sell their product or service once, have repeat customers, and get paid for it over and over. Other ways are property investors. Invest in a property, rent it out and collect the rental income each month. Do something once and get paid for it over and over. Do you get it? Take YouTube for another example; make a video once, get millions and billions of views and BOOM - YouTube sends you a paycheck. I won't go into the ins and outs of how to do any of this. That's a chapter for another day. This is merely just giving you a quick glimpse into the concepts of earned, portfolio, and passive income. There are huge tax incentives for people who own a business and investors too. Again, disclaimer here - seek professional advice from tax advisors. Not so much for employees, unfortunately, but employees get benefits in their jobs as well; paid leave, company car, health insurance, etc. Portfolio income is investing in something, waiting for it to go up in value and then selling it and making a gain on your initial investment. The stock market is good for this and property is too. A lot of people have this mentality in the stock market. Buy low, sell high and cash in on the profit.

I've followed these above principles - Time, Energy and Work - during times of adversity and it's gotten me through some tough times and my results in life show this. Remember what I said at the start of this chapter, some of us are closer to our death than to our birth. If that applies to you, I urge you to be bold, be courageous, and by all means, be YOU. Don't be lying on your deathbed many years from now regretting why you didn't take that opportunity, start that business, or make the investment. You can do it. Have a 'me too' attitude, follow the above principles, and you, too, will be fulfilling your dreams. Now is the time. Start now on your journey of overcoming adversity and becoming relentless in how you work. Work smarter, not harder. It's the difference in thinking that matters!

~ About Karl Davidson ~

Growing up, Karl followed the path that his parents and society told him was the right thing to do. He went to school, got good grades, and then went onto college. He achieved a degree in electrical engineering and got a safe, secure job. He did all this by the age of 20. Fast forward 4 years; he felt stuck. Stuck not in his job, which had flown him across the world to places such as Japan, United States, Taiwan and China, the Netherlands and which had him working on some of the most advanced machines in the semiconductor industry, but stuck in his own personal life. He was getting paid well, but had very little to show for it, except for some materialistic items. Karl had too much month at the end of his money and "Spending" was his middle name. He would buy things to fill the voids his life left open.

While on a job assignment in Japan, Karl was introduced to two books that would ultimately change his life. Little did he know these two books would open up the door to a whole new world that he knew existed, but didn't fully know and understand. One of these books was so powerful it stopped him *dead in his tracks* when he was crossing a street in a suburb of Japan. The other book was a personal finances book that educated him about money and wealth. During his travels and journey of entrepreneurship, he picked up a few core principles from various people and cultures he's been exposed to and used them to help shape and mold a winning recipe for success.

Once such thing was a Chinese proverb, "If someone gives you something and you benefit from it, you have a moral obligation to share it with others." This adage resonated so much with Karl that he has written about those things which have transformed mindset, and frequently shares them with others.

Karl has 10+ years of experience as a professional Semiconductor Engineer, working in places such as the USA, Germany, The Netherlands, Japan, China and Taiwan. He helps his clients get more financially educated through teaching courses. He is a precious metals investor, investing in gold and silver since 2018, and is an international property investor. Karl is a qualified NLP Master Practitioner. He facilitates a Facebook group with over 3K members called "Cashflow Club Ireland" and his Instagram page, with 6K followers, has been endorsed and recognised by Robert Kiyosaki. He is an author. He is a loving husband to his wife, Bronagh (Bron-na) and a doting father to his 6-month-old daughter, Brónadh (Bro-na).

The Positive Drip and Onyx Expressions Publishing, LLC

Presents

RELENTLESS

EMPOWERING STORIES OF OVERCOMING ADVERSITY

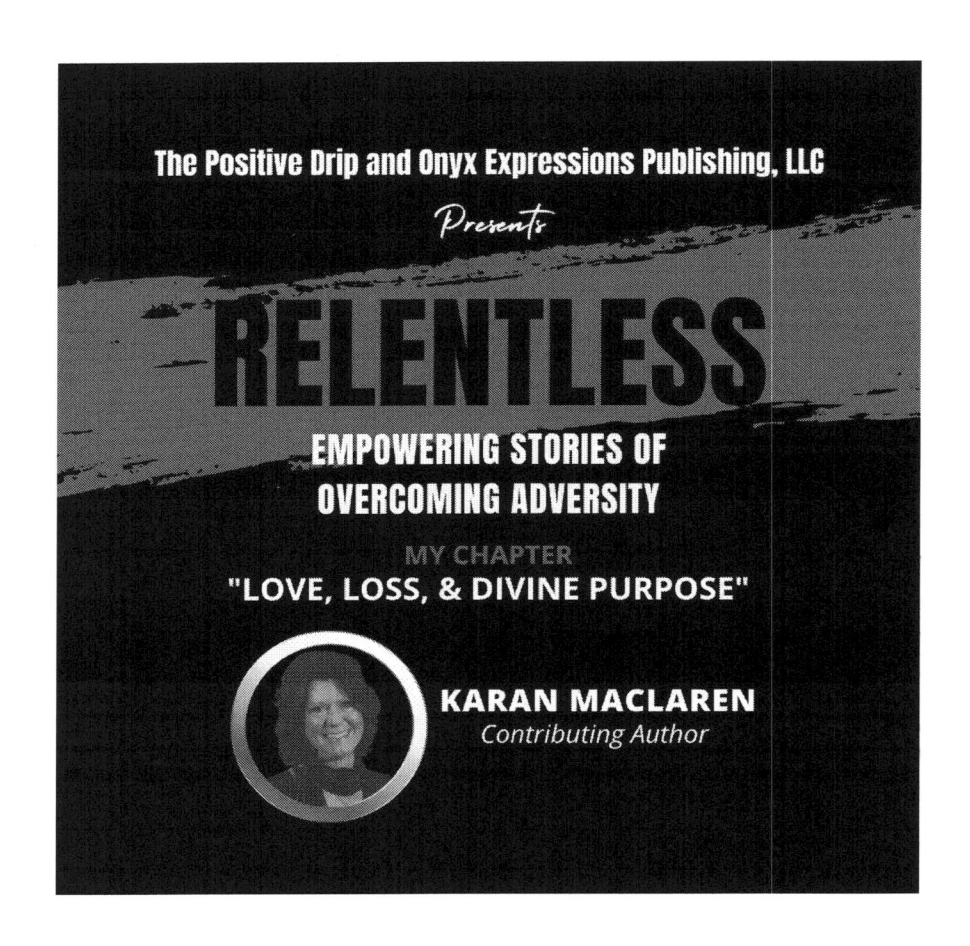

MY CHAPTER
"LOVE, LOSS, & DIVINE PURPOSE"

KARAN MACLAREN
Contributing Author

7:
Love, Loss, & Divine Purpose

By Karan MacLaren

Just another ordinary day at the bank. My desk is in the back, too far away from the door to let my co-workers in as they arrive, so I usually ignore the buzzer.

Not today though, for some reason I couldn't! I tried, but I heard it again. It didn't make any sense; my whole being was drawn to the door. Who was it?

A young man came in and was quickly whisked into the Manager's office.

I went back to my work, but had a hard time focusing. A while later, when he was being introduced to the other managers, I turned my head so I could see him. As he came into my section, he turned around to face me, and our eyes met.

We both held our gaze, unable to turn away. There was so much energy flowing between us and around us… it was so strong, the rest of the room melted away…It felt like we were the only two in the room. It was like we saw into each other's souls and a sense of knowing came over me. I knew I was supposed to know this man....

I came to realize that the universe put this man in my path because he was *the one*...the one I was supposed to share my life with, my soulmate.

We were living together within a few weeks and married 3 years after that.

We were poor, but happy, and a year later we welcomed a beautiful baby girl into our family. She was my world, my everything!

Soon, we were to be blessed with a second child. We couldn't be happier. This was my dream; a home and a family. Life was wonderful.

And then our world fell apart. I remember the last kick. My 3-year-old daughter and I were on the couch, playing, and I felt a strong kick from my unborn child. I remember the moment...and then silence.

The next day, I was more comfortable, but she was quiet.

My last doctor's appointment before her due date... I heard the two most dreaded words I had ever heard. "No heartbeat." As the doctor moved the monitor over my stomach, I did hear a heartbeat, but it was my own, not my daughter's.

I saw the doctor's expression change. She got me up and told me to get dressed and come into her office. She told me she couldn't hear the baby's heartbeat and was sending me for an ultrasound.

Off we went to get the ultrasound.

Started crying when I was changing, getting ready for the ultrasound. The technician heard me and came to see me. I told him... "No heartbeat." He took me right away and performed the ultrasound.

I could tell by the look on his face before he even said anything...no heartbeat.

They sent me back to my doctor's office. My husband was there...They must have called him.

The doctor took us into her office. She once again delivered those two dreadful words...no heartbeat. I told her I still felt movement. She said it was only Braxton Hicks contractions. I didn't believe her. She informed me that they would have to induce me. A date was set.

I was in denial... numb... speechless...

We went home to tell our families.

We told our daughter, and she was quiet for a moment. Then she starting laughing hysterically. It was so eerie. My husband told me he'd read that it was a child's way of dealing with bad news. He explained, they try to make it happier by laughing.

It broke my heart.

We decided on a name. We would name her Alexandra.

We were both numb. We tried to talk through the pain and anguish of the moment. We talked a bit and said we would try again to have another child. But first, I would have to give birth to Alexandra. Then, we would have to have a funeral before I could go forward. We realized that forward was the only way.

As we awaited the birth, I didn't believe the doctors. I felt her. I knew I did.

I was in denial all through delivery. I knew it was going to be a big mistake. In my mind, she was alive. I wanted to see her. We knew each other; we'd already spent 9 months together. You know your child; they're a part of you before they enter the world... Before they even take their first breath.

They were right. No heartbeat. No life. She was gone. Not even one day did I have with my beautiful baby girl. All the hopes and dreams I had for my baby, my child, my daughter…gone. I couldn't believe it. I never got to see her take a single breath.

She looked like me. She had my nose, my thin lips, the same dimple in her chin, and a few wisps of dark hair.

The nurse came in the next day. She empathized with me and said that no one knows how I feel but me, and not to let anyone tell me how I'm supposed to feel.

I so needed to hear that. I will never forget her. I held onto her words of comfort.

She was the angel I needed that day.

I went home, and I felt like I never wanted to go outside again. I wanted to hide from the world. But I had my three-year-old daughter to think of.

She saved me. She gave me a reason to carry on; a reason to get up in the morning. I had to get up for her. My beautiful girl… she was so good through it all.

Guilt becomes an ever-present emotion, even now. The questions keep showing up in my mind:

What did I do?

What didn't I do?

Why my child?

Was this punishment for some past sin?

Did she not want me for a mother?

Was I not worthy of her?

What am I lacking in?

Is it my fault?

And on and on. The questions never end.

I relive the nightmare every night before I go to sleep. This is how I keep her alive. Sleep doesn't come until the end of the story. Until I relive it all.

And then one morning, I realized I'd fallen asleep before the end. Oh, my goodness.

More guilt!!! How could I?

How awful of me to allow sleep to come?

What kind of mother am I?

I am forever and profoundly changed by the loss of her. I realize how fragile life is; how precious it is.

I remain in awe of how two people can come together for a few moments and their union can create another beautiful human. This perfect new life gives humanity another chance… A chance to do better…A chance to be better.

Our children come to us as a blank canvas. If we take the time and use the right brushes and apply the right colours, hopefully we can create a better version of ourselves. With that, we can create a better world for all of us to live in and especially for them to live in. This is the most important work we will ever do.

My child is gone, but how do I honour her?

How do I make her loss mean something?

I couldn't protect her, but maybe I can help protect other children.

Maybe somehow, someway, I can help make things better for them.

With that in mind, I became a founding member of a parent group dedicated to helping new parents. It felt good to be of help.

Time went by and we healed as a family. My daughter started school, and I started volunteering in her classroom. I loved it. I felt like I was giving back, paying it forward. When she was 5, we welcomed a baby boy into our family. I went back to volunteering, and he came with me into the classroom. The other children loved him and watched out for him and protected him. It was beautiful to watch.

I spent many years volunteering at the school. My heart was full. I felt like I was giving back, doing some good…honouring our child that was always with me, but not….

My children graduated, and my volunteering days came to an end. Hmmm. I thought to myself. What do I do next?

I've always been interested in nutrition, believing *we are what we eat*. And so, I decided to study Holistic Nutrition. The mind, body, spirit approach resonated with me.

I thought this would be another way for me to help people and to give back.

What I have discovered since becoming a Practitioner, is that so many people have emotional wounds that they carry with them. These wounds form the lens that they see the world through.

A person that carries grief, loss, betrayal, or any other kind of wound for a time will have it affect their physical health. Everything is connected.

One of the most important things I can do for a person is to create a place where they feel safe and cared for… A place that they can feel comfortable enough to open up and share their stories.

I find just the telling of their story can be healing. I don't have to do anything else. Just being in a heart centered place and listening is enough. This creates a trust and a bond between us and is the starting point for us to work together to heal not just the body, but the mind and spirit as well.

I know my darling baby girl, that I carry with me always, has guided me to this work.

If not for her loss, I may have chosen another path and that wouldn't have been the right path for me.

I'm doing what I am supposed to be doing... because of her.

Thank you, my darling, you will live on in my heart forever.

~ About Karan MacLaren ~

Karan MacLaren was blessed to have realized early on in life that one of the most important things, and one of the most rewarding things, is to be of service to others, especially for those in need. This fuels most everything she does. It's who she is.

Karan MacLaren is a Certified Holistic Nutritionist and a Certified Holistic Cancer Practitioner.

She was previously a Mortgage Specialist and Consumer Lender with one of the top Canadian Banks, but left her position to take care of her growing family.

She was an active volunteer at her children's school and served on the Parent Council in a number of different capacities over a 14-year period, acting as Chair, Vice Chair, Fundraising Coordinator and Snack Program Supervisor as well as sitting of the Staffing committee and the Nutrition Committee.

After her children graduated, she returned to school to study Holistic Health. After graduating from the Institute of Holistic Nutrition, she went into private practice, opening *KM Mind, Body, Spirit Wellness.*

Holistic Health embraces the mind, the body, and the spirit. Karan's goal is to provide a safe, caring place to foster trust and create a working relationship with her clients. She believes this is the foundation for working together to heal not only the body, but the mind and the spirit as well.

Karan works with clients to help identify the root causes of their health issues using symptomatology, and then creates personalized protocols tailored to their specific needs, including appropriate lifestyle changes that support the mind and the spirit as well as the body.

Karan believes that health is the foundation of everything and without it, we can't hope to achieve any of our life goals.

"Health is a state of complete physical, mental and social well-being and not merely the absence of disease or infirmity."

For a complimentary list of foundational health guidelines for cancer or any health concern, please contact Karan at: kmmindbodyspirit@gmail.com and please insert "Relentless" in the subject title.

Karan MacLaren looks forward to helping you on your path to wellness.

The Positive Drip and Onyx Expressions Publishing, LLC
Presents
RELENTLESS
EMPOWERING STORIES OF
OVERCOMING ADVERSITY
MY CHAPTER
"A CAT WITH NINE LIVES"
FRANKIE KINGTON
Contributing Author

8:
A Cat With Nine Lives
By Frankie Kington

Have you ever felt like a cat with nine lives? You are probably thinking, what does Frankie mean by this? Well then, have there been events in your life where you have thought to yourself 'My, oh my, that was a close shave.' Maybe these incidents were a matter of life and death experiences or maybe they were things that helped you realize that you needed to make some changes in the direction your life was headed. As I reflect on my life, I realize that I have experienced many of these such events in my life which I now look at as my "nine lives," which we affectionately attribute to cats.

The first one was in 1979. I was playing out in Ardwick Green at the back of my flat. Did you know I stood on the copper bar inside a concrete slab and, to my surprise, I slipped off this bar and it banged me straight in the face. My face was throbbing, and it swelled up because of the force of it hitting my face. It could have done a lot more damage, but thankfully, I survived.

The second incident happened in 1981. While in secondary school, I was playing a game on the playground. As I jumped over a wall to grab my friend, I slipped and banged my leg and shinbone. My friends carried me into the Headteacher's room, where I waited with blood gushing out of my shinbone. The scene was horrific. I was lucky I didn't do more damage to my leg. I was taken to hospital and ended up having several stitches.

The third incident took place in 1982. I used to go swimming in a park near my house in Gorton, called Debdale Park. My friends and I decided to go for a swim to the yacht in the middle of the reservoir. Halfway there, I lost my breath and started panicking. My friends tried to calm me down, but I continued to struggle for breath and thrashed around in the water. Fortunately, the driver of a speedboat saw me panicking and my friends trying to calm me down. He pulled me out of the water and took me back to the shore. I could have drowned that day.

The fourth incident was in 1984. I used to hang out in Stockport with my friends, where we got friendly with a couple of guys we used to drink with. We ended up meeting some girls in Stockport, and to our surprise, we weren't liked by a group of lads down there. One night they decided to jump me and our friends in the Stockport town centre. One of my friends was punched in the face by a guy who had knuckle dusters on his hand. This marked my friend's face badly and left blood gushing from his head. By this time, the fight had spilled out onto the road. There was a bus moving in my direction, but luckily for me, I managed to dodge it by pulling my head back and throwing my body down onto the pavement. "That was a close encounter," I said to myself as my back slammed into the concrete.

The fifth incident was in 1985. I was being racially abused, and I reacted. Before I knew it, I had gotten into a fight with a guy. I punched him and he went straight through a shop window. Even though this was an accident, that I didn't mean, I was still quite lucky to escape that situation.

The sixth incident also happened in 1985. A friend of mine was sniffing glue one night on Gorton Market, near where I lived. For some reason, I decided to try it. After a few hours, I realized this wasn't a nice experience at all and decided I didn't want to do that again. Gas, I found, was more enjoyable. It gave me a funny, buzzing sensation, and seemed much more controllable. Fortunately, this was a brief addiction that didn't last very long either. I knew it wasn't good for me at all. It made me dizzy, dazed and confused. Both these situations could have resulted in more dangerous consequences.

The seventh incident was three years later - in 1988. By this time, I had become addicted to Speed (Amphetamines). It got to the point where I was in injecting drugs into my arms. Obviously, this is a very dangerous way to abuse drugs; if you use dirty needles, it can cause septicaemia, known as blood poisoning. You never know what is in the powder: it could be rat poisoning, washing up liquid or flour, because some drug dealers may just want your money. So, you have to trust it is the drug you ordered. If not, it could cause an overdose or even death. I was very fortunate that this did not happen to me.

The eighth incident took place in 1992, near where I lived in Clayton. I was sitting in my mate's car when a man smashed the car window with a stick. The glass shattered in my face but, luckily for me, no serious harm was done. No shards were stuck in my skin and I did not have any gashes on my face or neck. Of course, I was a little shaken up, but again, I survived. This incident could have been a lot more dangerous.

The ninth incident happened in 1996. I took crack cocaine, which is a dangerously and psychologically addictive drug. The reason I took this drug was I was grieving for my uncle who had died of a brain haemorrhage while at his girlfriend's house in Gorton, the United Kingdom. I looked for relief from my grief and chose to cope with this sad situation by taking crack cocaine. This addiction lasted for one year until I finally decided to stop taking and start thinking more of my Uncle Eddie. Even though he was no longer here, I knew he would not have been proud of me at all. I dug deep and thankfully, found all the strength I could arouse to get myself clean and off drugs.

I remembered all these incidents very clearly because any of these events certainly could have killed me or caused big effects in my life. I am sure I could have touched on some more events in my life from which I had a narrow escape. Even during my school years, I was bullied and got into several fights, but I always came out unscathed and victorious.

Through all these incidents, I always felt like there was something telling me about my life. I want to teach people that no matter how far you feel you have fallen, there is always a solution to every problem if you take the right actions and ask for help.

Growing up in Manchester, I had to be streetwise because it wasn't an easy place to live. However, I felt I had a reason to be here, other than just getting high, drinking and using drugs, and blaming the world for my problems. I needed to get away from feeling like the victim and start taking full responsibility for my life. I decided to transform my life.

My first decision to completely transform my life was to go back to Education in 1997 at the age of 27. My dad advised me to go into the world of Information Technology (IT) to learn computer programming. So, I started my first course in Computer Programming at a Mancat College of Arts and Technology - or Mancat for short... I was really excited to be going back to school to learn Computers, but there was a problem. Initially, I found it quite difficult to learn. Even more difficult was seeing and knowing there were students who didn't seem to care about their education. It was frustrating because they were messing about all the time. They were talking loudly and sitting on the desktops where the computer keyboards were stationed. Instead of working as they should have been, they were playing games on the computers. Unfortunately, my teacher wasn't the best, and I ended up making complaints. Despite my complaints, I left with nothing - no certification at all. Undoubtedly, this college experience wasn't as good as it could have been, but I used it as a stepping stone to do bigger things in IT.

As the next step on my IT journey, I enrolled in a C.O.B.O.L. Computer Programming online course at Computeach Learning, an IT Training company. C.O.B.O.L, which is an abbreviation for Common - Business - Orientated- Language. This was a more difficult course, however, I managed to pass two courses in Computer Programming. They were Diploma and City & Guilds Standard Certifications. At some stage, I was wondering whether Computer Programming was what I really wanted to do, because I couldn't find work no matter how hard I tried. So, I went to pursue a Computer Networking course in Salford, United Kingdom where I learnt a lot more about computers. I worked in Salford for 12 months and then worked at Fujitsu for three months. Did I like it? No, I didn't. I am not criticising the companies, I just felt they weren't for me. Eventually, I decided to move away from working with computers.

So, I decided I would like to work for a company named 'Stand-guide'. This was a great company where I learnt so much about myself. In my role as a Placement Officer, I worked with various organisations to place students in temporary positions at different companies. The students' roles were either professional work experience or internships. This job led me to better and more interesting job and career opportunities.

I even had six months' experience working as a Civil Servant for the Job centre. That was quite an experience. The stress levels were so high that if the health and safety officers had visited, they would have closed the place down. It was not a good working environment. Arranging direct payments into a customer's bank accounts over the phone proved to be much more challenging than I had imagined.

Funny enough, after that job, I ended up being a Security Officer for the largest security firm in the world, G4S. I had the responsibility of changing light bulbs, fixing plug sockets, mending damaged furniture, putting up signage in corridor areas of the building, and reporting odd jobs which needed doing. Soon thereafter, I was offered a position in Management, which I gladly accepted. This led me to acquire some very useful skills, including Customer Service, Customer Care, Conflict Management, and First Aid, which gave me the tools I needed to effectively deal with all types of people.

The lessons I have learnt are about building your strength and character through overcoming hardships. The ups and downs can really strengthen your ability to win through any situation and make you a more balanced and determined person to be successful in your life.

~ About Frankie Kington ~

Frankie Kington experimented with smoking cannabis, injecting amphetamines known as speed, and taking other drugs during his turbulent teenage years. As a young adult, he felt a sense of hopelessness which led him to smoke crack cocaine.

Despite all the challenges he faced, Frankie turned his life around and found value and a true purpose. His love of learning led him on a variety of paths before he decided to pursue his passion for mentoring and inspiring young people.

Frankie changed from a troublesome kid to a successful entrepreneur. Let him take you on his journey from addiction to enlightenment and show you how he turned his life around. He succeeded against all the odds with its inspiring message of hope.

Frankie Kington is an entrepreneur, mentor and public speaker, known as The Wise Entrepreneur. He is passionate about helping and inspiring young people to fulfil their true potential and to avoid the mistakes he made in his youth.

Frankie nurtures young people's skills and encourages them to overcome the obstacles they inevitably encounter. He empowers young people to make the most of the opportunities open to them and to realize that achieving goals and dreams is possible for everyone, no matter what background they come from or how much money they have.

He shares his own powerful story openly in the belief that it will prevent young people from getting caught up in drug abuse, alcohol addiction or violence and crime.

His mission is to empower one million young people to become inspiring entrepreneurs and thought leaders in society over the next 30 years.

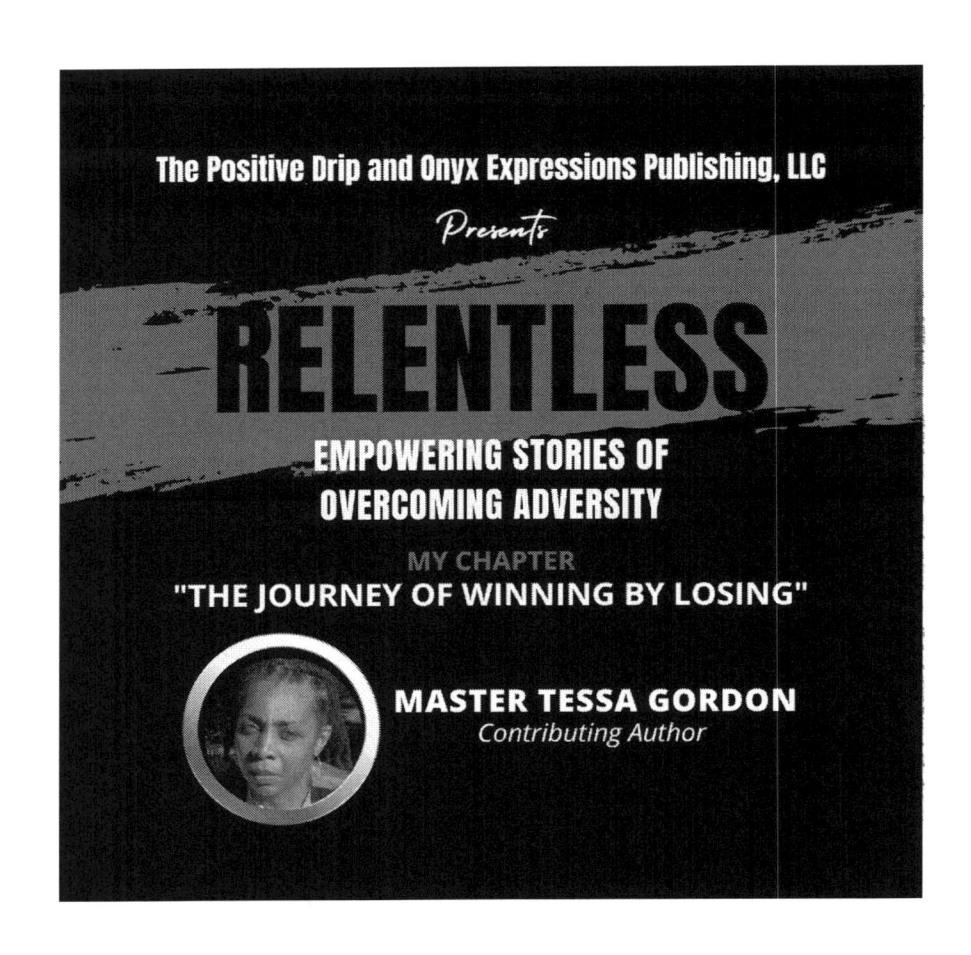

The Positive Drip and Onyx Expressions Publishing, LLC

Presents

RELENTLESS

EMPOWERING STORIES OF OVERCOMING ADVERSITY

MY CHAPTER
"THE JOURNEY OF WINNING BY LOSING"

MASTER TESSA GORDON
Contributing Author

9: The Journey of Winning By Losing

By Master Tessa Gordon

"**C**an't" is a word that's not allowed in the Mamba Martial Arts Studio. The reason this is so important for me is that I know how limiting beliefs can impact our overall wellbeing and self-esteem. Even though I've been winning since I was 9 or 10 years-old, I know how it feels to lose. It's a terrible feeling that we have to learn to shake-off. If we aren't careful, it can consume us and really attack our self-confidence. Some losses land differently. I know this from personal experience...

It was 1988 when I got my first taste of defeat. That bitter taste was so bad that it sometimes still haunts me, now decades later. It was the first time that Tae Kwon Do was introduced to the Olympics as a demonstration sport. I had worked really hard and trained my entire athletic career for this moment. I had won many competitions; both at home in Canada and many international ones too. I was excited and nervous all at the same time. I suffered terribly with insomnia and often trained at 2:00 a.m. I was always working out - and stressed out! Now, here I was in Korea at the World Tae Kwon Do Championships and headed to the Olympics in Seoul, Korea. I was 21 years-old and among the most elite athletes. It was a great experience. Just being there amongst the best of the best gave me a rush of adrenaline.

I was psyched and pumped up until the night before when one of my coaches pulled a straw and got Korea - just my luck. Here I was on the mat facing my opponent, a Korean fighter who was on her home turf. I couldn't believe it. Of all the straws I could've pulled, I pulled Korea. At that moment, it didn't matter to me that I beat Korea in 1985. All I could think of was that I was now on her home turf. We went back and forth for three extremely intense rounds. It was so close that no one could even guess who was going to be the victor. In the end, sadly, victory was not mine on this day. It was not my hand that was raised to claim any medal... no gold, no silver, not even bronze. At first, I was excited to see my fellow athletes walking around with medals hanging around their necks. Then, it became difficult to see them because I had to face the fact that I was going home without one. I was stunned as I made that seemingly endless, lonely walk back to the locker room. I was devastated. I couldn't believe it. I had never experienced elimination in the first round. I sat there thinking, "Do I retire or still chase my dreams for gold in 1992?" I returned home to Canada and did everything I could to push through the heavy feeling I had picked up from Korea. I felt depressed and anxious. I couldn't shake the feeling like I wasn't good enough. I was just going through the motions, barely functioning. I knew I had to do something... I just wasn't sure what I needed to do.

It was April 1992, and I had to make one of the toughest decisions of my life; should I maintain my amateur status in Canada or head to the United States? The 1992 Olympic Games were being held in Barcelona, Spain.

The gold medal was calling my name, but so was my desire to become an instructor of high demand. I longed to pursue my professional goals outside of actual competition. I decided to take a quick trip to New York to visit my cousin, who lived in Brooklyn. I had competed there and enjoyed visiting, but had no desire to live there. I literally had $100 in my pocket and knew it would be a short trip before I returned to Toronto. Even though I was 25 years-old, it felt like I was running away from home. Being there, out of the spotlight of my hometown, was refreshing. I really liked feeling like I could breathe again. Since my immediate family was still in Canada, I found that I liked the freedom of being by myself. It was a feeling I couldn't really explain. It wasn't long after I decided I would apply for my green card. Even though I was a gold-carded athlete, had a lawyer and all the documents I needed to apply as an "Athlete With Extraordinary Ability," I was initially denied. I thought to myself, "It's ok; I've been here before." I decided I would not allow this disappointment to defeat me - again.

In the end, that internal voice won out and so did I. At first, I began teaching privately out of my apartment. I couldn't let go of the feeling I had back at home in Toronto when I was teaching martial arts to students with disabilities. I fell in love with this experience. I was especially rewarded whenever they hung in there and learned the skill I was teaching them. It was even more incredible because sometimes it took as much as three times longer for them to get it than it did for my students without disabilities. After I realized that I loved what I was doing and I was really good at it, in fact, I was one of the best, I opened my own studio in Park Slope, a "small town" neighborhood in Brooklyn, NY. I was again blessed with having the experience of teaching students with disabilities. One truly amazing experience I had was teaching a student who was blind.

Working with someone without sight is challenging, yet very gratifying when they are able to execute what I've taught them!

My studio, once named *Pure Energy Martial Arts* was renamed to *Mamba Martial Arts Studio* following the Covid shutdown. I am very intentional about pouring 100% into my students. Proudly, I have touched the lives of hundreds of students. I developed an acronym to help remind them to do what it takes to face their challenges head-on and persevere through everything that comes their way. **D.R.O.P.** is a quick, easy way to remember the core pillars of finding success in sports and in life as well. **D**iscipline. **R**espect. **O**pen-mindedness. **P**ositivity. When they keep **D.R.O.P.** at the forefront of their everyday routines, they are bound to achieve anything they set out to do. At any given moment, life can collapse around us and make us feel like giving up. We all go through challenges in life. We can be at the top of our game, no matter what it is and it can collapse at any given time. With the right attitude and a commitment to never giving up, you can work your way up again.

I am a firm believer that my faith and connection to God has made me strong and sustained me through every one of my life's challenges... Yes, even that dreadful loss decades ago that has helped me win at life today! I love what I do and I know I am making a difference in the lives of children and adults as they journey through life navigating losses and gaining the confidence they need to win, even when they lose. That loss that I thought was going to destroy me was the very thing that caused me to discover the greatness within me and become the person I am today. I teach each of my students to become the best version of themselves. I help them to search inside and find their greatness. Everyone has greatness within. I found my greatness as I discovered my business, which turned out to be my life's mission.

When it came to opening my business, nothing was easy, and I quickly realized nothing is given to us on a golden platter. Earned accomplishment can never be taken away. I learned that high-level achievement cost and the price I had to pay was in sweat, blood, time, tears, doubt, and commitment. One of my biggest lessons was to seek help from others. Don't be afraid to ask for help. I came to realize that I had endless support from my peers, family, friends, and most of all, my founding students from 31 years ago who have played a significant part in doing what I am doing today. If my fear was greater than my need to ask for help, I would not be where I am today…Impacting the world.

Belief in yourself has to be so big that it is greater than any doubt that could ever enter your brain. Even though I had doubts in myself, I hung onto the belief that others had in me to keep going and to keep pushing forward. I went to work and implemented my D.R.O.P. plan and philosophy. Believe it or not, it's the minor things that make the biggest differences. Perseverance is the key to a positive outcome. D.R.O.P. everything and NEVER GIVE UP!

I was intentional and made it my business to get in alignment with my Father's business! I am grateful to have the opportunity to serve every day and have a profound impact on my community. Remember, I've been there - I used my greatest loss to become my greater win!! My journey to winning would not have happened without my loss. We just have to use our inner D.R.O.P. until we uncover it, embrace it, and bring it to life! It may look like we are walking alone, but as it is written in the poem, **"Footprints In The Sand,"** it is really God who was carrying me the whole time. I love being in a position where I can carry my fellow students through aspects of their lives. We are all students of life and we should be grateful to lift up and carry others when we can because we never know when someone will have to do the same for us. I would love to help you do just that. If you are interested, please reach out to me and let's make it happen!!!

~ About Master Tessa Gordon ~

Originally from Toronto, Canada, Master Tessa Gordon holds a 6th degree black belt in the Korean art of Tae Kwon Do. Gordon was a member of the 1988 Canadian Olympic Team, nine-time Canadian National Champion, World Championship Medalist and Pan American Champion. Today, Gordon has been practicing Tae Kwon Do for over 35 years.

As a young child, Gordon began training in basic kicking and punching techniques at home. As her progress and enjoyment of the art became evident, her parents enrolled her in the Jong Park Institute of Tae Kwon Do. She found the discipline required for traditional training incredibly demanding both emotionally and physically. Yet with the encouragement of her parents, she continued to train.

As Gordon advanced in rank, she began to fall in love with art of Tae Kwon Do. Tae Kwon Do became her way of life. By the age of 12, she was a black belt. At the age of 13, and for the next three years beginning in 1980, Gordon was rated Canada's number one female point fighter in open competition where all martial arts are represented. She was the youngest woman point fighter in Canada fighting in the adult women's division. She was also the first Canadian, male or female, to be included among the top ten fighters rated in the North American Karate Circuit.

In 1985, Canadian women were chosen to compete in the world Tae Kwon Do Championships for the first time. Gordon was one of the first chosen for the team and was a Canadian National Team member from 1985-1988. Some of the highlights of her many accomplishments around the world include winning the bronze medal at the 1985 World Champion ships in Seoul, Korea, the gold medal at the 1986 Pan American Games in Quayaquil, Ecuador, silver medal at the 1987 World Championships in Barcelona, Spain and the silver medal at the 1988 Pan American Games in Lima, Peru. Her most valued experience, however, was competing for Canada in the 1988 Olympic Games in Seoul, Korea.

The Positive Drip and Onyx Expressions Publishing, LLC

Presents

RELENTLESS

EMPOWERING STORIES OF OVERCOMING ADVERSITY

MY CHAPTER
"THIS PUSH IS FOR YOU, MOMMA"

MICHAEL CLAYBORN
Contributing Author

10:
This Push is for You, Momma

By Michael Clayborn

Trials come at a most inconvenient moment. They are always unexpected and are strategically placed to make your life uncomfortable. That discomfort is not to make you quit; it is only there to make you transition into your next phase of life. Every victorious outcome came after the conflict. There is no problem you face in life that isn't already designed for you to win. I know that seems irrational, but I encourage you to do something, trust God when you're afraid, when you're unsure, and even when you don't see a positive outcome. Even though I know this is the truth, to be honest, I didn't always feel like believing it. Keeping it real, I was so angry with God, that trust wasn't exactly on my mind. I felt betrayed by God when His purpose overruled my own.

Typically, if mom called my two siblings and I to a conference call, there was something on her mind. Most conference calls, the three of us would do a decent job of being receptive to what Momma had to say. This call was different. She told us something I never expected to hear. My mom was our shero. Not too much shook her, but today was different. I could hear the trepidation in her voice. I could tell this call was hard for her. It felt different. I listened intently as she spoke. After all, I was the oldest of my mother's three children, and the family expected me to be the voice of reason and the leader. Even though I knew I didn't always get it right, one thing I knew for sure was that I was going to be there. Everyone relied on me. There was a certain confidence that came along with being the family's superhero. I was the backbone of the family and everybody knew the Mike would be there, no matter what. She was doing her best to stay calm and sound as strong as she possibly could, but I could hear the worry and fear in her voice as she gave us her doctor's diagnosis. Momma was diagnosed with stage four ovarian cancer. This was the beginning of many heavy conversations.

Like most solo superheroes, in the same capacity that you trust you can fix everything, you can also wear the cape of failure. My cape of failure was invisible to the naked eye, but it was definitely there. Even though our loved ones don't see the cape, we still know it's there. I vividly remember how I felt when I returned a missed call from my mother. Momma told me that she'd called me while she was on her way to the hospital. My heart sank. Immediately, I felt like I had failed. I felt like she had to experience that traumatic event alone. Little did I know, missing Momma's phone call was just the beginning. What was to follow would change our lives forever. That sinking feeling would show up later.

Still to this day, one of the hardest things I've ever had to do was accept the fact that my mother, my shero, was dying. The words that came out of my mouth next shocked me. "Momma, I think you should just take your pain medicine and live." Without hesitation, all of mom's children jumped right into action. The journey had begun. Through countless appointments, multiple surgeries, and a lot of physical changes, we saw momma go from superwoman to a superwoman on steroids. Momma was already an unstoppable, relentless woman. She was incredibly strong. It seemed like when she received the cancer diagnosis, she morphed into superhero overload. Momma began to travel more, had become more independent, and was more eager to see the world by experiencing things she had only dreamed of experiencing.

You would think that after uttering those words of acceptance of my mother's diagnosis and the inevitable, I had come to peace with the fact that she was dying. On the contrary, I now realize that moment of peace was just that, a moment. I saw Momma's pain and wanted to give her what I thought would make her live out the rest of her life happily and excitingly. So, I planned this long list of things that we'd do together. One of the reasons I re-enlisted into the Army in the first place, was my mother. I knew the military would move my family and take us to some cool places all over the world. I wanted my mom to be a part of those wonderful experiences.

My beautiful mother, my angel, Vera Clayborn, lost her battle with cancer in March 2019. My siblings and I had put a lot of effort into taking care of our mother. To me, it wasn't fair. Losing my mom is still one of the most hurtful things I have ever had to experience. When Momma passed away, I felt like God could have at least allowed me an opportunity to check a few more boxes off of my to do list. I was hurt! I was angry! I was bitter, and eventually fell into depression. If I may be honest, that's a hurt that never goes away. I was mad that He didn't give me a chance to check off all the boxes. It hurt me to my core.

My entire world was completely shattered. Even though I had a family of my own, momma's passing left me feeling as if I had lost my purpose. I felt that I had no real reason to remain progressive in life. Then came the funeral. After all the time, effort, and other resources spent to take care of mom, it had led us to a hurtful end. My siblings and I had never left Momma's side. Now, here we are having to leave Momma in a cold, dark, lonely place... the grave. That day, we both entered the same dark place...the sunken place. That sinking feeling returned. It was heavy and deep in my heart. Every time it resurfaced, I did my bet to push it back down.

I had always known about depression and had even been the catalyst for others' recovery from depression. I had never experienced depression on this level. So, I did as any other A- personality person would do, mask it. My imposture syndrome levels were at an all-time high. I masked my hurt by staying busy. I enrolled into college, continued my transition into the active duty Army, I began motivational speaking, my children were always involved in some type of sports event, etc. My wife and I even opened a business. My family and I relocated from Memphis, TN to Georgia and eventually from Georgia to Colorado. Busy, busy, busy. Not to mention we had just had our third child. Whew...This new busy was my way of not thinking about Momma. It was only when I was alone and about to go to sleep that I would notice I had fallen into a depressed state. To me, my reason to function was gone. It was buried in the cemetery. My antidote to the late-night deep thoughts, however, was late-night gym sessions. I would work out for two hours late at night to suppress my emotions. This helped me sleep at night. I didn't have a workout plan, nor did I follow any routines or programs. I would literally just workout until I didn't hurt anymore, or I was simply too fatigued to continue. Sounds like I had it figured out, right? I thought so too.

Upon my arrival at my first duty station, we received orders to deploy for nine months. I did like a typical soldier does and kiss their loved one with a long, see you later kiss. Me, thinking that I would be able to continue my "busy" routines to suppress these untreated emotions, deployed with the same thought process. Little did I know, that I was actually being pulled away from my busy lifestyle, and in some sense, isolated to be healed. Now, this may seem like an oxymoron and the wrong answer for a person who was actively suffering from depression. In the Bible, Paul was isolated on an island to receive a mission from God. I later discovered that I was, too. Deployed and in a foreign country, I continued my routine. After long work days, nothing would stop me from my two-hour gym sessions. One day I was in the gym, I began to cry. Not realizing what was going on, I quickly wiped my face and continued my workout. Another day I go to the gym, and more tears began to flow. I simply wiped my face as before and continued my workout. Tears would continue to come more days to follow, only these other times, I would have to leave the gym, go to the restroom, and cry. Sometimes I would return to the gym and other days, I wouldn't. It was then that my "200lbs of shredded muscle self," finally accepted the fact that I needed help.

With this escalating, now aggressive, internal battle going on inside, I was still reluctant to go to counseling. God has a strategic way of letting you know that you are not alone in battles we face. Traci Logan, a longtime friend of mine and my wife's, had just published a book entitled, "Your Grief Ain't Like Mine, And That's Ok". It wasn't how the book read that persuaded me, it was what the book told me to do. Within the pages of the book, I found both instructions and solutions. In following the directions, I had to write down exactly how I felt. WOW! I had never physically expressed how I felt. After reading Traci's book and confiding in a few of the soldiers I deployed with, I took the first step and walked into a counselor's office. I was at an isolated moment, away from my family and my normal busy lifestyle, when God showed me that I was in the right place for an emotional healing. Almost the moment I sat down in the chair to speak, every emotion I had been suppressing came out at one time. I could barely speak for crying so much. The release I gave that day was life changing. It was even more phenomenal because I walked into that therapist's office just days before the two-year anniversary of my mother's death. I had never accepted the fact that what I needed to heal was a grief counselor.

Today, I still grieve for my mom. However, I refer back to three principles my counselor instructed me to always remember; 1. It's ok and healthy to release; 2. It's okay to seek help; and when you get done releasing that emotional pressure and frequenting your counselor, keep moving. These principles are still applicable in my life. I've learned that even Superman needed a shoulder to cry on from time-to-time. Because I took the leap of faith into unfamiliar territory, I found my healing. Using these simple principles, I not only help myself but others who are experiencing a tough season in their lives. With the help of God, my beautiful family, Porsha, Malachi, Gabrielle, and Myles, and a strong support team, I would not have been able to overcome.

Even though Momma did her best to prepare us for this, she didn't tell me it would be this hard. I wasn't ready for all of the pain that it brought or for all of the work it would take to heal. I had to trust Him with tears in my eyes, hurt in my heart, and with a depressed state of mind. Once I allowed myself to heal, my purpose was redefined. I still had loved ones here with me that were depending on me to succeed. I still push for my mother, but I also push for my family, and more importantly, for myself. So, if you don't want to push for yourself, push for those that love and support you. Just keep pushing, you've got this. This push is for you, Momma.

~ About Michael Clayborn ~

In the small hospital, of the small town of Hayti, MO, Michael Clayborn was born to the late Charlie and Vera Clayborn. As a child, Michael learned servitude from the examples his parents set for his brother, Kevin, sister Kendra, and for himself. As Pentecostal pastors, community activists, and as entrepreneurs, Charlie and Vera taught Michael and his siblings the importance of having a strong relationship with God, a good work ethic, and a healthy relationship with the people you serve. These principles are what have shaped Michael's character today.

After graduating from Hayti High School, Michael moved to Tennessee, where he began a career as a Correctional Officer. Always hungry for the next level of success, Michael later began a new career as a Police Officer. From the Basic Police Officer's Training Academy, he enlisted into the United States Army Reserve as a Combat Engineer, and went to basic training at Fort Leonard Wood, MO. Within the nine years as a law enforcement officer and eight years as an Army Reservist, Michael faced an enormous number of challenges to include the cancer diagnosis of both of his parents.

Married to his wife, Porsha, for 13 years, Michael discovered that Porsha and their three beautiful children Malachi Tyre, Gabrielle Aniyah, and Myles Tyre, were what redefined his purpose after the passing of his parents. Michael overcame these adversities by remembering his reason for starting his success journey.

Michael re-enlisted in the Army under an active-duty contract and enrolled as a full-time student at Lakewood University for a Bachelor of Science in Information and Technology. Michael hosted the Inspirational and Motivational talk show "Lunch With MicSi" and is actively aspiring to turn that talk show into a podcast. Michael has traveled to multiple cities to speak to elementary and high schools.

Michael has also used his story to inspire others at community functions, churches, motivational stages, etc. Michael believes that if by using his story could save one person, then that is one person closer to reaching their maximum potential.

The Positive Drip and Onyx Expressions Publishing, LLC

Presents

RELENTLESS

EMPOWERING STORIES OF OVERCOMING ADVERSITY

MY CHAPTER
"BREAKING THE CYCLE: EMPOWERING WOMEN TO FIND THEIR PATH TO REDEMPTION"

DAWN LONG
Contributing Author

11:
Breaking the Cycle:
Empowering Women to Find Their Path to Redemption
BY DAWN LONG

The sun is shining as I drive down a curvy highway. This is a joy to drive if you like taking the curves a little tight. I'm going to Farmington, MO in August, in the middle of the longest heatwave and drought that the Midwest has suffered from in a while. Yes, it was quite hot, but none of that really mattered to me because I had my husband by my side. It was the happiest drive that we had together in a long time. We were singing (subjective - lol) and just bursting with joy and impatience to do what we wanted to do for a long time. This drive was different. It was not like the last drive we took to Farmington in the winter, when we had to drive away without our son.

That day in August we were actually driving to Farmington to bring our son home after a long 5 plus years that he was away. Why was our youngest of 3 sons away from us for that long? He was in prison for a crime he committed. Let me take you back to that day when our world turned upside down and sideways. Our lives were changed forever.

I remember it was right after a tornado touched down about six miles away from our community. I had to stay late that day at work to complete a homework assignment for my *Data Analytics* class. Since the internet was down from the tornado, I used the work office to upload my work. If I had not stayed late, I would have arrived to my home being raided by the US Marshalls.

My middle son called me as I was driving home and let me know that my youngest son had been arrested. I was in that foggy, hazy tunnel of you may be able to relate to - the one when everything just slows down to a crawl. All I heard was the *woosh* of my heartbeat as it sank and raced at the same time. As I pulled up the driveway, I could smell the just fresh cut grass, my husband had done before he had gone to work that day. I barely remember opening the car door and petting our two dogs and walking up the deck to an open front door. I stepped inside where it was dim and I could see my house turned upside down from the raid. I picked up the warrant as I read it, I remember starting to shake and crying as I read the charges and what they were looking for. My bedroom was tossed, but not as bad as the rest of the house. I realized that I nor my family would ever be the same after that. Hard-drives gone with the last pictures of my Mom before she passed and the memorial PowerPoint we made for her. Gone were all the childhood pictures of our boys, never to be seen again. Just like my hope for this world was gone in that instant, I thought I would never have those family photos again.

For months, I *broke down* at work at the drop of a hat. I went to every hearing just to hear the judge tell my son how vile he was. The darkness during that period was all-consuming. There was no light, and I felt like I was underwater for most of it. My husband was angry, so angry that he dropped down to 145 lbs. This was too thin for a 6-foot man. His doctor was concerned, and so was I. The anger was literally eating away at the love of my life.

I decided, then and there, that we were going to pull out of this and work on us. We needed our relationship to survive and our sons still needed their parents, even though they were grown men. How did I do that? I did it with the help and support of an amazing group of women that I happened to meet during a women's conference in Tennessee.

We all settled in and started to get to know each other that evening and we had a little game where there were women lined up on two sides of the room and the person on the end started going diagonal to the person across from them and whispered something that they noticed about that particular woman. There were over 15 of us. Do you know every single woman that whispered in my ear said, "You are the light." Mind you, up to that point, none of us really knew each other. We were strangers. No one knew what each person was going to say. There were four women there that I knew from another group, but not on a personal level. I got chills, and I asked the universe what was the meaning of this? "I am light to what, exactly?"

One other person that was there with me knew something was going on. We had a chat later that night. We will call her "Ellie." Ellie and I discovered we had some things in common. As we talked she said, "You need to tell your story because so many other women go through this too." Another woman chimed in the next day and told me the same thing. Is this where our healing begins, I asked myself? Can I do this? It turns out, yes, I could and I am doing it.

I started to notice that there were other moms in the groups I was in and they were struggling with the same thing I was. My family was with having justice impacted loved ones that were either currently incarcerated or were previously incarcerated. I saw a pattern amongst us. I realized it was that very pattern that was something we could work together to change. The change I am talking about is breaking the negative generational patterns that got us there in the first place.

When I started uncovering and diving into the various negative patterns, I recognized that we were stuck. It seemed like we were unable to break free from the destructive habits and thoughts that had consumed a part of our lives. I saw women who were tired of feeling stuck and powerless. They were desperate to change their lives for the better. I began to understand what negative patterns are and how those patterns affect our lives. Once I could identify the specific negative patterns in my own life, I was able to understand the causes and triggers of those patterns.

The next step was learning how to break the cycle. How did I do that? I found techniques for interrupting those patterns and created a practice of identifying positive replacement behaviors. One of those techniques is something you can do anywhere, anytime; it is singing! Yes, singing. Remember, at the beginning of this chapter, I said I was singing? This was why. It helps break that negative community in your brain to get it to quit yammering. Why does this work? Because it is a brain disruptor. This disruptor throws your brain off of the merry-go-round of that negative tape that is twirling in our minds.

What about positive replacement behaviors? How did I take the negative and replace it with the positive? I did it by starting small and making a new habit that I could do along with what I was already doing. For example, we have a morning routine, right? What can you add to your morning that you can build on? What habit did I add to mine? I added, saying three positive affirmations before I even got out of bed. Every morning when I miss saying them, I notice that it throws my day off. For me, this is a practice that helps me tremendously.

What I want you to take away from this is that your life can change. Your life is not static. You can do the hard things just like I did. Has it been easy? No. But anything we do in life worth the reward is worth doing the hard things that it takes to get the rewards. It is worth turning your waiting room into a classroom. It is worth working through the days that looked like the worst days of your life. I speak to you as a mom, a wife, a *Nana*, and an animal lover, and I want you to know that you are loved. You are unstoppable and you are a beacon of hope. Give me your hand and I will walk with you through the fire. I know the way, my love. Together, we will come out on the other side, stronger than you or anyone ever imagined.

~ About Dawn Long ~

Dawn Long holds a Master's degree in Leadership and Management, and is a certified Human Resources professional. She has over 20 years in the retail arena with some of the largest companies in the US. As a proud mom of three boys, a loving wife, and a doting Nana to her grandchildren, family is everything to Dawn. She also has a furry friend who is incredibly spoiled and brings me endless joy.

In addition to her personal roles, She is also a Transformation Life Coach and podcaster who specializes in helping people break negative patterns in their lives. Whether it's overcoming limiting beliefs, developing a growth mindset, or improving relationships, Dawn's goal is to empower her clients to achieve their full potential and live their best lives. She is passionate about helping others and believes that with the right mindset and support, anything is possible.

She is happy to share with you a free workbook, "Breaking Negative Generational Patterns: A Transformational Guide". This workbook is designed to help you identify and break free from negative patterns that have been passed down through your family for generations.

Inside, you'll find a step-by-step process for examining your family's history and identifying patterns that may be holding you back in your personal and professional life. You'll also find practical exercises and tools to help you develop new, positive habits and build a life that aligns with your goals and values.

With this workbook, you'll gain a deeper understanding of the impact that generational patterns can have on your life, and how to break free from them to create a better future for yourself and your family.

To get your free copy of "Breaking Negative Patterns: A Transformational Guide", and a 30 min free coaching call, simply enter your email address on Dawn's website or email her and it will be sent directly to your inbox. She also offers a paid course that is yours for a discount of 50% off the normal price. She is excited for you to start your journey towards a more fulfilling and empowered life.

The Positive Drip and Onyx Expressions Publishing, LLC

Presents

RELENTLESS

EMPOWERING STORIES OF OVERCOMING ADVERSITY

MY CHAPTER
"FROM STRUGGLES TO STRENGTH: THE GIFT OF RESILIENCE"

FLEX MARKS
Contributing Author

12:
From Struggles to Strength: The Gift of Resilience

By Flex Marks

Adversity is an inevitable part of life. It can come in many forms, from personal struggles to unexpected challenges in the workplace, home, and personal life. Regardless of the type of adversity, it can be difficult to navigate and overcome. For some, it may feel like they are lost at times. In this chapter, I will share a significant episode of adversity that I encountered and experienced head-on, and the lessons I learned from it.

Coming from a 25-year coaching background, I've always informed my clients about how to listen to their body; the signs and signals it gives to them. Unfortunately, for the first time in my life, I wasn't practicing what I preached. In late 2010, I was rocking and rolling. I had a very successful personal training company, and I had just built a state-of-the-art, personal training website. My dream was to coach people worldwide. I also had partnered with my best friend to launch our film and video production company. I was in the best shape of my life. I was training five times a week, eating clean and getting rest....or so I thought. By the summer of

2011, something started to happen. I was feeling run down. I began to experience extreme fatigue, headaches, and other physical symptoms. These symptoms made it challenging for me to focus on my training and work. My body was failing, and I wasn't listening to it. When I started putting on weight, I began to train twice a day. I began taking pre-workout supplements with caffeine to help boost my lacking energy. I got more strict with my diet and started eliminating my salt intake. However, nothing seemed to be working. I lost a ton of strength and struggled to perform 8 pushups. Within 3 months, I had put on 30lbs. My body temperature had dropped by 2 degrees. Things were definitely not adding up.

After a doctor's visit and some tests, I received a devastating diagnosis. I was told I was "fine and healthy." WHAT??? According to my blood work, I was fine. I knew in my heart something was wrong. This didn't sit well for me. I knew my body was fighting something and that blood work made zero sense to me. I decided to see a naturopathic doctor. Just from my first visit with my naturopathic doctor, I realized that I was in for a pretty tough fight. I had developed extreme adrenal fatigue. All the signs were there. I wasn't allowing my body and mind to rest. I was diagnosed with a chronic autoimmune disorder. The diagnosis hit me hard. I was scared, confused, and overwhelmed. I couldn't understand how this could be happening to me, and I began to feel like a failure. One thing that did put my mind at ease was that my naturopathic doctor said, "Even though it's chronic right now, we can fix it." However, it could take up to several years, depending on how severe the adrenal fatigue is. In case you're not sure what adrenal fatigue is, I'll explain very quickly. On top of your kidneys lie two organs called the adrenals. They are responsible for everything such as your hormones, enzymes, thyroid function, and controlling body temperature. It's basically your *fight-or-flight* organ of the body. It also controls cortisol, which is a hormone. Cortisol is a stress hormone that causes a lot of these issues: weight gain, brain fog, lack of energy, aging, and pretty much everything that I was going through. So, with that in mind, I'm sure you can understand my concern.

So, the plan now was to get my adrenals stronger, control my cortisol levels, and strengthen my gut lining. Due to my body temperature having dropped by two degrees, my gut and my stomach had gotten cold and damp. When that happens, the body's immunity starts to really get affected. The stomach contains 80% of the body's immunity.

One of the biggest issues was that my stomach lining was compromised. I had developed *leaky gut syndrome*, which is basically small tiny holes in the stomach, where food can leak out right into your bloodstream. Unbeknownst to most of us, 80% of the population now has leaky gut syndrome and has no idea. The bottom line was, I didn't listen to my body. I was over-training and manipulating my diet with little or no salt. The pre-workout supplements I was taking added to the problem. My adrenals got weaker and weaker until they finally just gave up.

At this point in my life, I was actually taking more supplements to help with my chronic illness than when I was training. I didn't care to train anymore, and I didn't even care to coach anymore. I was in a new field, the film industry. Making more money than I ever had and felt very successful at what we were doing. However, still in the back of my mind, I knew that 'Flex' Marks no longer existed. I was okay with that for a bit, however, every so often I'd be on the video set with some Olympic athlete and they would always ask why my nickname was 'Flex.' I don't always tell them the full story of what happened to me, instead I show them old photos of me. I felt like that was just a different part of my life. Then one day, I got a really rude awakening.

One of my closest friends, a very dear friend that I have known for over 20 years, was battling a much bigger fight than I could ever imagine. I've admired my friend Nelson ever since meeting him when I was 14 years old. He orchestrated and advocated for me to get hired at our local community center, which ended up being a huge part of my life then and still is today. This was when 'Flex' Marks was born. I loved coaching, I loved teaching, I loved my community and this all stems from that one day where my friend, Nelson, approached me and said, "You need to work here". Unfortunately, five years ago, Nelson was diagnosed with cancer. Long story short, almost every doctor had written him off. He fought through it and reached out to me during his treatment. We reconnected and vowed to each other that he would beat this cancer thing and I was going to help him.

I experienced cancer with my mom, Elly-May Marks. She was diagnosed with breast cancer in 2002. She was in remission for 2 years and then got diagnosed with a brain tumor and passed away within 60 days of that last diagnosis. I understood where Nelson was coming from and I wanted to do whatever I could to help him. One day during one of Nelson's hospital trips, something told me to stop feeling sorry for myself. I decided to get off my ass and actually do something to win my life back. It was a day I'll never forget. I was with Nelson at one of his appointments and he was learning to walk. He'd been in a wheelchair for over a year and all he wanted to do was just walk again. Here I am watching one of my best friends learning to walk as I sat in a chair, 70 lbs. overweight, and feeling sorry for myself. That day ended with me declaring, "ENOUGH IS ENOUGH!"

At that time, I wasn't even thinking about going back to coaching. I just wanted to feel better and not be this sad, depressed person. I'm watching my friend recover from this life-threatening battle, something he didn't do to himself. That next day I started to train again. I took it slowly and made some changes in my life. I had to clear my mind of negativity, which was hard. That meant I had to let go of some things and some people in my life that I felt were just pulling me down. There were a few things that I needed to do and a few steps that I needed to take. Some things I had learned in the past while others I had to really incorporate and start practicing them. Despite feeling discouraged, I decided to face the adversity head-on. I took some steps to manage my stress and anxiety by practicing mindfulness and engaging in regular exercise. I realized there were some new lessons I needed to teach myself and embrace.

The first lesson I learned was the importance of accepting reality. Denial can be a powerful coping mechanism, but it can also prevent us from moving forward. It's important to acknowledge and accept the situation, no matter how difficult it may be. Once I accepted my diagnosis, I was able to focus on finding ways to manage my symptoms and continue pursuing my goals.

The second lesson I learned was the importance of asking for help. Adversity can be isolating, but it's crucial to reach out to others for support. I reached out to my family, friends, and a great naturopathic doctor for help, and their support was invaluable. They provided emotional support, helped me manage my symptoms, and encouraged me to keep going.

The third lesson I learned was the importance of prioritizing self-care. It's easy to prioritize external goals and forget about our own well-being. However, self-care is crucial, especially during times of adversity. I began to prioritize sleep, exercise, and a healthy diet, which helped me manage my symptoms and improve my overall well-being.

The fourth lesson I learned was the importance of cultivating resilience. Adversity can be difficult, but it can also build strength and resilience. I learned that setbacks and failures are not the end, but rather an opportunity to learn and grow. Cultivating resilience helped me stay motivated and optimistic, even during challenging times.

The fifth lesson I learned was the importance of staying focused on my goals. Adversity can be distracting, and it can be easy to lose sight of what's important. However, by staying focused on my goals, I was able to stay motivated and continue pursuing my dreams. I learned to break my goals down into smaller, more manageable steps, which made them more achievable. I realized that consistency trumps perfection. So, I remained diligent and consistent.

After applying these principles and lessons to my life, I was able to overcome my severe adrenal fatigue and thrive. Although my chronic autoimmune disorder is still a part of my life, I have learned to manage my symptoms and continue pursuing my goals. Now, the best part I'm going to share with you, I've left for last. Once I dropped that 70 lbs., and got the zest for life back, I realized I could help more people than before. Enter... *The Freak Squad Training*. I sat down and wrote out, in detail, what I had done and the steps I had taken to execute my comeback. I knew men over 40-years-old were suffering from what I had suffered. I had developed an immunity to training and nutrition. I had finally broken free from my body, being immune to everything. I had newfound knowledge, and I wanted to share it with hundreds and hundreds of other men in their 40s suffering from adrenal fatigue and training immunity. So, after putting pen to paper, it was time to build out a proper strength training, nutrition and mindset program for men. This was the chance for me to train people from all over the world. Within one year, I had my very own online strength and muscle building program up and running. As of today, I'm humbled and honored to train hundreds of men from all over the world; changing their lives for the better. Who could ask for anything more?

In conclusion, adversity is a part of life, but it doesn't have to define us. By accepting reality, asking for help, prioritizing self-care, cultivating resilience, and staying focused on our goals, we can overcome adversity and thrive. From all of that, we can develop resilience, strength, and a strong growth mindset that will serve us well in all areas of life. The plan that I used to overcome my adversity is one that most any over 40-year-old man can do and it will change his life forever. After the medical crises and adversity that Nelson and I experienced, I feel absolutely humbled and responsible to help as many men as I possibly can. So, if you are a 40+ year-old man, not quite feeling at your optimum, and want a few tips on how to enhance your physical life, please reach out to me so we can explore whether or not my plan would work for you. Let's overcome adversity and redefine life.

~ About Flex Marks ~

Flex Marks, also known as Jay Marks, is a Certified Strength and Condition Coach hailing from Toronto, Ontario. From a young age, Flex was fascinated with exercise, and his interest only grew after receiving a Hulk Hogan Workout Set when he was just ten years old. As a teenager, he found himself competing in Kickboxing and even became a Kickboxing coach at the local community center.

Flex was determined to take on new challenges and expand his knowledge, so he became a Certified Coach/Trainer and eventually became the Head Trainer at Extreme Fitness, one of Toronto's top fitness gyms. After three and a half years, he decided to start his own coaching business and has since helped thousands of men in their 30s, 40s, 50s, and beyond build muscle, lose weight, and get stronger.

Through his online Strength and Muscle building program, Freak Squad Training, Flex teaches men how to overcome "Training Immunity" and take control of their health and lifestyle.

His five "demandments" of training, nutrition, recovery, and mindset have helped his clients achieve their dream physiques and maintain them. Flex Marks is a true leader in the fitness industry and is dedicated to helping others live their best lives.

As a thank you for your time, Flex is offering you a Free 90-day subscription to Freak Squad Training.

Please visit Flex's website at: http://www.freakmusclebuilding.com/

The Positive Drip and Onyx Expressions Publishing, LLC

Presents

RELENTLESS

EMPOWERING STORIES OF OVERCOMING ADVERSITY

MY CHAPTER
"LIFE IS A SERIES OF THIN THREADS"

LINDSAY CRUZ
Contributing Author

13:
Life is a Series of Thin Threads

BY LINDSAY CRUZ

The truth is, we are all "one" decision away from living a completely different life. I truly believe this is the case.

It's April 7, 2023 and here I sit, neck deep in numbers, building a career and running my own business in the Financial Literacy realm. I sometimes pinch myself to check and see if I'm only dreaming of where I am today or if I'm actually really here. Don't get me wrong, I'm still not where I'd like to ultimately be. However, there's one thing that I do know for sure; nothing comes easy. "Success" doesn't happen overnight. As I sit here staring out of my window admiring my Canadian view, I can not help but remember how and where my story of chasing ambition started.

Being the eldest of four children, I could see, remember, and understand what my parents were going through firsthand. I was in elementary school when my father decided to work abroad, in Korea, in order to sustain the needs of our family back in the Philippines. Sacrificing not seeing us till I graduated high school, our parents, having a glimpse of a brighter future for us, made another huge step to switch roles and my mom went on her way to work in Hong Kong and then ultimately in Canada.

Graduating with a degree in Communications in 2017, I was set to pursue the career I loved, excited to put myself out in the field and build the life I wanted for myself back in the Philippines. I had this bubble filled with dreams and goals until we got the big news that we are moving to Canada. I knew it was part of my parents' plan, but I did not realize that it was going to happen so soon. I knew they had plans to move to a new country for better opportunities and a chance for a better life for all of us. But what about *MY* plans?

Fast forward to when we landed in Canada as immigrants. I remember thinking I felt like I was a newborn baby being in a new country, where we knew absolutely nothing about it. From using the transit, to applying for apartment rentals, and looking for jobs, we dealt with changes and had to adjust to a very different and diverse environment.

Despite all the hurdles, we were blessed to have each other and family friends who helped and guided us. We were able to calibrate in no time! I accepted the fact that this was our new home. I asked myself, if I were to stay here long term, what would I want my life to look like?

Remember when I said I had recently graduated from university? I found out that it is not good here; meaning I have to go back to school in order for me to pursue the career I thought I wanted. I was devastated. I had been studying most of my life and at that time, I thought going back to school again would be a *waste of time*. But, did I let that stop me from dreaming again? Absolutely not. I decided to use it as an opportunity instead of an obstacle. I asked myself, "What do I want to be? Where do I want to go?" I am a firm believer that every person in this world is meant to do something special; something uniquely theirs to do. We all have a purpose. I started thinking about traveling a lot, having control of my time, and helping other people in any way possible.

I knew the importance of education, but instead of enrolling for the next semester, I entertained opportunities that could help me achieve and create what I thought a quality life would look like. I learned to be resourceful and to work with whatever tools I had. I was open-minded to every door that was available to me. I was optimistic. I saw the good in the bad. I had always been interested in meeting new people.

One day, as I came home from work, my parents were talking to an accountant who said she could help us buy a house. As new immigrants, a couple of banks declined our applications. We were just told to pay off our debts, have higher income, and build our credit scores without even explaining how. Then there's this lady explaining how doable it is for us. To this day, I believe it was fate that our paths crossed because I asked her to teach me what she does. She taught me and I went on to get a license and eventually joined her brokerage. That's how it all began for me. I leveled up my association in the field and fell in love with it at the same time!

Do you recall that famous question from when we were kids? "What do you want to be when you grow up?" How many of you ended up being who you wanted to be? I've always wanted to be a teacher. I admire my teachers and see them as heroes who are molding us to be great individuals in the future. But that changed one day when my mom asked me if I wanted to be like the reporter on TV. She also knew I was very talkative. I thought, wow, I want to be seen on TV and be famous! That is how I chose a program related to media and it is also because I wanted to avoid math so badly. I loved writing essays and public speaking, but I didn't do well with numbers. Isn't that ironic? I have been working in the financial industry since 2018 and I love it!

Looking back and realizing where I am now is what made me think that change really is the only constant in life. I am associated with a team of financial advisors whose mission is to leave no family behind. Running my own business, building my own team, being financially literate, I was able to share what I know with my own family and fellow Canadians. From where they can put their savings, being financially protected, to buying a house. I am just starting, but I've never been more passionate and happy with what I do...I am a teacher - molding the financial futures of those I teach about finances!! Not the kind of teacher I originally envisioned, yet a teacher that is making a difference in the futures of people. To those people, I am their hero!

Life did not turn out as what I initially planned it to be, but I had faith in the process and made the most out of it. Change is inevitable, but so is making a decision. When it starts raining hard, do you just stay home and not go to work? When you find out you are sick, do you just sit and not see a doctor? When my dreams were knocked out after graduation, did I just cry and blame my parents? No. I became very intentional about what I did. I didn't give up. I kept pushing forward. I realized that life is a series of thin threads...they all work together to sew the pattern of our journey.

Having to experience what I went through, I have learned important lessons that I always take with me.

1. Have a positive and tough mindset. Instead of asking, "Why is this happening TO me?", ask "Why is this happening FOR me?". Switch your mindset and get the job done. Adversities are part of the journey. You can be disappointed with an outcome, but DO NOT GIVE UP.

2. Believe in yourself. Have a belief that others can borrow. At the end of the day, it is just you. Nobody is gonna come and rescue you. I always remember, if it's meant to be, it's up to me!

3. Surround yourself with the right people. Never take advice from someone you don't want to switch lives with. Be around individuals who have 1 & 2.

Learning from my mistakes and still continuing to be a student of life, I know there will be more adversities ahead. But with the right mindset, confidence, and the right people around me, I know it will be more manageable.

This is just the beginning. Sowing a seed will create a bountiful harvest! Thread the needle of life and start sewing...one thin thread at a time creates a beautiful quilt!

~ About Lindsay Cruz ~

Lindsay Cruz is an entrepreneur based in Toronto, Canada, focused on helping her clients achieve their financial goals. Moving to a new country after she graduated with a degree in Communications in the Philippines, she found herself in the world of finance. Although somewhat new in the industry, her passion for entrepreneurship and helping families be financially educated is far bigger than her lack of time served in the industry. She is relentless!

As financial advisor, Lindsay realized that in finance, what we don't know can hurt us. Hearing different stories and having her own experience of not knowing what to do when in financial trouble is what motivated her to be open-minded and learn about finances. She believes that education and experience are two things that nobody can take away from her and that the same is true for you. This is why she is diligent in teaching her clients vital information about finances. As she started her journey in financial education, she focused on helping herself and her family to get ahead in one of the richest countries in the world. Once that was fulfilled, she started guiding clients on where to invest their savings, educating them about the proper financial foundation, and helping them move to their first home. Lindsay believes if her family can do it, yours can too!

Knowing what she knows now, Lindsay concentrates on her mission of leaving no family behind. Being able to see her clients be more financially aware, she is more intentional in every move she makes. It is not always easy. She uses her personal experience with naysayers, doubters and adversities as her fuel to help others overcome their challenges. The satisfaction of seeing her clients be in a better position is weighs more than anything in her career. It is priceless!

You can reach Lindsay at lindsayanncruz@gmail.com or on her personal Instagram account @lindsayanncruz. Use the code word "relentless". She looks forward to connecting with you!

The Positive Drip and Onyx Expressions Publishing, LLC

Presents

RELENTLESS

EMPOWERING STORIES OF OVERCOMING ADVERSITY

MY CHAPTER
"WORK/LIFE BALANCE IS BULLSH*T"

JUSTIN SMITH
Contributing Author

14: Work/ Life Balance is Bullsh*t

BY JUSTIN SMITH

WORK-LIFE BALANCE IS BULLSHIT.

Did that get your attention? Good. That's why I led with it. For me, work-life balance is an illusion, and striving toward this elusive goal would cause me more harm than good.

Now, I'm over it. Let me tell you why.

Since I was a wee lad, I knew what I wanted to do when I grew up. I was always fascinated with the power of storytelling. The ability to communicate with others through stories is one of the most ancient and powerful human forms of connection.

My love for storytelling was innate, and I brought that energy to the work I did in school.

In grade 3, I wrote a book that my teacher adored. So much so that she read it to the entire class. In grade 7, I won the gold medal in my school's public speaking competition. At the end of my junior high term, I was recognized for my storytelling. I was enrolled in a unique arts program that combined classical mediums with up-and-coming media formats.

This is where I fell in love with video. I found telling stories through the medium came naturally. This discovery inspired me to build a career in this field.

After high school, I began an upward trajectory. I was building my video-producing skills and reputation. I started small, but landed bigger jobs with brands (like Pepsi, Canadian Tire, Tim Hortons, and Microsoft).

These brands had sizable budgets. They would spend money producing the content and had dollars to throw behind marketing. Which meant my stories got out into the world and connected with audiences.

My childhood dreams were coming true!

Balancing work and life was easy because work was life. I was the centre of my universe, and (minus some quality time with my wife) I could spend all my time pushing forward my ambitions and dreams.

Everything was going great, and my success felt like it was moving at light speed.

That was until the accident that completely derailed my career.

The accident was 6 pounds and 7 ounces, and he was the most beautiful thing I had ever seen in my entire life.

On July 21, 2014, we welcomed Noah Zachary Smith into the world, and, like all parents, he completely changed my life for better... and for worse.

That's right, worse too.

I think it's tough for parents to admit this publicly. It's much easier (and trendier) to post photos of happy family moments on whatever social media platform you're into and wait for the likes and positive comments to roll in.

But in quiet moments with enough prodding, parents will admit (right after saying it's magical and incredibly rewarding) that it's also de-railed their lives.

They are right. Being a parent is magical. I love my kids (yes, we had a second) and being a great parent is as important to me (if not more critical) than success in my career. That being said, it's crucial to recognize that a healthy and fulfilling life requires attention to family and work ambitions.

My friends who are parents (and there are not many) and I joke that being a parent while attempting career success is comparable to playing life on hard mode. If you have more than three kids, we say it's playing life on extra hard.

Being a parent while attempting to grow a successful career comes with many challenges.

CHILDREN'S NEEDS ARE UNPREDICTABLE AND WILL CHANGE RAPIDLY.

Social norms and expectations pressure parents to prioritize their families over work responsibilities.

Technology and work's "always-on" nature may make it difficult to unplug and fully disengage from work-related responsibilities.

Many jobs require long hours or may not offer the flexibility to adjust work schedules to accommodate family needs.

Parents can also feel guilty or conflicted about taking time away from work to focus on their work or personal lives.

Now, more than ever before, being a parent makes achieving career success difficult. There is more competition in the workforce than in previous generations, thanks to globalization and the ability to work remotely. In previous generations, when work was hyperlocalized, fewer individuals were competing for your position because the talent pool was much smaller.

Now the competition is millions or more. Many competitors are younger or cheaper (or even free - think of how advanced AI is, and it's getting smarter by the day!).

The only way to win is to outwork these folks. That's hard to do when you've taken a massive chunk of your workdays and weekends because you also decided to take on a second job: being a great parent.

What makes a 'great parent' has changed since the previous generation. Being a great parent today requires different skills than previous generations due to the changes in our social norms.

A parent is no longer expected to simply provide for and leave the kids to their own devices. Today, there is a greater emphasis on spending quality time to build a child's self-esteem, as opposed to the authoritarian parenting styles that were more common in previous generations.

I think almost all parents (I say 'almost' because I can't speak for everyone) want to be great parents. So, mailing it in isn't an option.

With the need to excel at work and parenting, this is where the idea of work-life balance comes into play. How do you balance work and life so your career and relationships with your children thrive?

My answer, learned through countless attempts to create balance, is you don't.

Trying to optimize for and manage a consistent work-life balance structure didn't work for me. I'm guessing, it probably won't work for you, either.

I'm happy that my career and relationships with my children are going well. My job is still on an incline (not as fast as I would like, but it is what it is), and my kids and I connect deeply almost daily.

That being said, my career and relationships with my kids are imperfect. They are full of dynamic challenges that change daily.

There is no getting over these challenges. Parenting is an infinite game (if you don't know it, please look up the term), and although it's difficult, it keeps life exciting. It's meaningful and rewarding.

SO, WHAT HAVE I LEARNED SPECIFICALLY? LET ME TELL YOU.

But before I give out unsolicited advice, I want to preface that although my career and parenting are not perfect (and never will be), I am surviving one of life's most difficult challenges.

First, I realized that being a good parent required me to be very selective in what I took on. I learned to prioritize and compartmentalize my life. Accepting that I couldn't do everything and that some things had to take a backseat was essential. I had to choose what was most important and learn to be okay with the rest.

I also had to learn to trust the process and trust myself. I had to believe everything would work out, even when things were chaotic (which is all the time). I learned to take things on faith, even if I didn't have all the answers.

I had to understand that constraints could be helpful. When I accepted that I couldn't do everything, it helped me to focus on what was most important. It allowed me to be more productive and do the things that mattered most.

Most importantly, for fellow high achievers, you can't beat yourself up when you're not at your best. It will be awhile (if ever) before you get to that state again. When your attention is divided, you must manage your expectations of what is possible. Be kinder to yourself and don't expect to be the workaholic that you were pre-childbirth.

The key to success when balancing work and parenthood is to be selective, prioritize, and to compartmentalize. Remember to trust yourself, have faith, and accept that almost always, less is more. This way, we can become better parents and better businesspeople.

Now go out there and do your best. Be a great parent and elevate your career.

Stop worrying about work-life balance because it's bullshit. Am I right?

~ About Justin Smith ~

Justin Brennon Smith was born in 1984 and raised in Toronto, Ontario, Canada. He's a loving husband and proud father of 2 rambunctious young boys.

When he's not busy working or doing his fatherly duties, you can find him consuming all types of art (movies, books, podcasts, concerts, video games, plays, tattoos, art galleries, etc.), lifting heavy weights, dreaming of travelling, and laughing over dinner and drinks with friends.

From creating elaborate storylines with his action figures as a kid to writing books and comics in his early youth to graduating from the Northview CyberArts program, Justin is a lifelong creative. His love for cinema was inspired by classic 90 films, such as The Matrix, Pulp Fiction, 12 Moneys, The Usual Suspects, Being John Malkovich, and Fargo. Justin attended York University and graduated with a BA in Film Theory.

At the age of 23, Justin started his career by diving head-first into the video industry. He founded BizMedia, a creative video agency focused on creating video content for the web, specifically for new-age (at the time) social platforms like Facebook, Instagram, and YouTube. The company gained notoriety through innovative storytelling, working on cool ads with brands like Coca-Cola, Airmiles, Samsung, Microsoft, and Mattel.

A jack of all trades, Justin has worn every hat in the video production book. He loves the creative process from start to finish, from producing, writing, directing, shooting, editing, colouring, and sound mixing.

BizMedia was recently acquired by Pixel Dreams (another fantastic Toronto creative agency). Justin is currently the head of the video production division at Pixel Dreams. He spends his days being creative while building the video department, one shot at a time.

If you want to connect with Justin, please reach out. He doesn't use social media for his personal life, so it's best to email him at...

Work: play@pixeldreams.com

Personal: justinbrennonsmith@gmail.com

The Positive Drip and Onyx Expressions Publishing, LLC
Presents
RELENTLESS
EMPOWERING STORIES OF
OVERCOMING ADVERSITY
MY CHAPTER
"CASTLE IN THE SAND"
MEAGHAN TANAKA
Contributing Author

15:
Castle in the Sand

By Meaghan Tanaka

When I was 19 years old, I died. My heart kept beating and my neurons kept firing, but I ceased to live. For more than two years, I was crippled by major depression. I slept 16 to 20 hours almost every day. When I was not sleeping, I laid in bed, willing myself to fall back asleep, to return to the land of the dead, a place where I was free from the thoughts and feelings of self-hatred that tortured me when I was awake. I wanted my existence to end, but just as I lacked the energy and motivation to socialize or study, I did not have the volition necessary to end my life.

What caused this deep depression? Was it the death of a loved one? A bad breakup? Financial ruin? A serious illness? None of the above. There was no trauma or tragedy. My life was good, and I knew it. I felt undeserving of all the good things in my life and became overwhelmed by guilt for squandering my gifts and failing to realize my potential.

Throughout my life, I was always able to achieve more than most of my peers with minimal effort, but I never set goals or strove to excel. As an obedient only child in a middle-class family, I was put on a path to university. I meandered along it without seriously considering where it would lead or how I would get there. At the end of secondary school, I picked a program on a whim and attended classes in my usual desultory fashion. Before starting university, I only wanted to get a Bachelor's degree, but once there I found myself immersed in a collective consciousness of inadequacy. I learned an undergraduate education was useless. Without a graduate degree, I would be unemployable, but my marks were not good enough to get into graduate school. I was a failure at university, so I was doomed to be a failure for the rest of my life.

The path I was on had disappeared and I could not see any other routes. I felt there was no way to go back and no way to go forward. Although I had never been truly confident, I went from feeling satisfied with doing "enough" and being "enough" to feeling insufficient, inadequate, and utterly lost. My sense of self was demolished.

Years later and after much introspection, I came to realize that before this existential crisis, my sense of self had been a castle of sand. It had been fragile and foundationless, molded by my parents' fears and insecurities. Waters of self-doubt, self-hatred, and loneliness had eroded it for years without my awareness. When the wave of inadequacy hit me in university, it washed away my sense of self completely. I had no resilience to rebuild it. Instead, I dug down and withdrew further and further. The world above shrank to a tiny circle of gray sky.

There was no one to pull me out of the pit I had dug. I lived with my parents, but they could not see a way to help besides trying to fill the hole, which only buried me. I was a skilled con artist who always met my commitments and hid my problems from my friends and coworkers. So, I languished in my pit for more than two years. Then one day I went into my school registrar's office and said I needed help. There was no epiphany or inspiration. I simply decided I could not go on like I had been and since suicide was not an option — my death would kill my parents — I had to get help. The decision was simple, but the action was not. It took countless attempts to get help. Most attempts ended before I made it out from under my duvet.

My first conversations with the registrar and the counsellor they connected me to were physically painful. I never asked anyone for help and admitting I needed it felt like an evisceration. All the thoughts and emotions I had tried to avoid poured out of me at once. It was like I had finally dug so deep I had hit groundwater. All the assumptions, doubts, and fears that had always permeated my life were pooling at the surface. I analyzed and traced them back to their sources: some I inherited, others I absorbed, and others were taught. I came to understand that those waters would always be there, but I also learned how the tides and rainfalls in my life affected them. With the help of a counsellor, my aimless digging became mining. It took years, but I found the resources I needed to turn sand into concrete and I slowly engineered a new castle with deep and strong foundations.

It needs regular inspections and maintenance, but twenty years later, my castle is standing strong and always expanding. I work as a counsellor now helping others when they have experienced trauma or a tragic event. I would like to share with you 6 fundamentals for coping with and hopefully conquering depression. I offer these not as a counsellor, but as an individual who used to wish for death and now lives not only a happy but a joyful life.

KNOW THAT YOU ARE DESERVING.

Believing that you are deserving is essential to recovery. When you are depressed, negative thoughts and emotions of inadequacy, guilt, and worthlessness ensnare you. These are all related to feeling undeserving. You can feel undeserving of not only happiness but also undeserving of depression.

The first thing you need to understand is that you cannot "deserve" to be depressed. When you have to endure a tragic or traumatic experience — such as the loss of a loved one, a job, or a relationship — it is a normal response to feel sadness and grief. This is not depression. Depression is when your life is relatively good, but you have lost the ability to find interest or enjoyment in it.

The second thing you need to understand is that to get better, you need to want to get better and you need to believe you deserve to get better. This seems obvious, but many people do not improve even with medical treatment because there is some part of them that does not want to get better or does not believe they deserve to get better. This is not just my opinion; research has shown it (Zimmerman, 2022). If even a tiny part of you feels undeserving of recovery, you must work to understand and resolve it.

PRACTICE SELF-COMPASSION.

Most of us try to be kind and supportive of our friends when they are struggling. We listen and we offer words of reassurance and encouragement. However, when we are struggling — regardless of whether it is from feeling inadequate, choices we have made, or events beyond our control — we rarely treat ourselves with the same gentleness and compassion.

Part of feeling deserving is learning to stop judging, criticizing, and condemning yourself. Self-compassion is about using mindfulness to be present with your emotions without judgment so that you can recognize when you need support. The easiest way to practice self-compassion is to imagine your best friend was in your situation. Treat yourself with the same compassion you would show them. Research has shown that self-compassion offers the same benefits of self-esteem — less depression and anxiety — but with none of the downsides and more stability (Neff, 2023).

DO NOT COMPARE YOURSELF TO OTHERS.

This book is full of "success" stories written by people who not only survived but thrived after facing adversity. When you are depressed, you can be so consumed by negative feelings of worthlessness, shame, and guilt that stories intended to inspire can have the opposite effect. Reading them can be a form of social comparison that heightens your feelings of inadequacy and being undeserving. If you are already struggling with unhelpful patterns of thinking, be wary of comparing yourself to anyone else, including the authors in this book. Everyone is running their own race or on their own journey, whichever metaphor you prefer. We all have different start and end points. We are taking different routes and facing different obstacles.

Do not compare yourself to others. Compare yourself only to your past self and celebrate any progress you have made. When you look at others, do not judge whether they are doing better or worse than you; focus on what you can learn from them.

Meaghan Tanaka

KEEP MOVING FORWARD.

The Chinese philosopher, Lao Tzu, said, "The journey of a thousand miles begins with one step." No matter how long and difficult the journey or race ahead of you may seem, focus on taking one step forward. When you are in crisis, that step may simply be breathing and staying alive one more day, hour, or minute. Keep scaling down until you find a step you can manage. Once you have managed that, do it again.

FIND THE SUN.

Even if you are not struggling with depression, it is easy to see all the things that are "wrong" in the world. Stories of tragedy, suffering, and violence dominate the news. It can be hard not to despair when all you see are dark clouds looming. Remember that even on the most overcast day, somewhere above those gray clouds, there are blue skies and beautiful sun. Find the sun. Find the good in each day. Find beauty and wonder in the everyday.

CONNECT WITH OTHERS.

In Western societies, individual strength is valued. There are negative connotations about relying on others, but something magical happens when you reach out to others and open yourself up to them. When you admit vulnerability to others, you create a safe place for them to do the same. It allows you to connect to them and through them, to the universe, to something infinite. You find help and support you did not know existed and you see how you can help others, which studies show is incredibly beneficial for your mental health. Research shows that helping others increases feelings of well-being, encourages you to be more active, expands your social networks and skills, improves self-esteem, and can even create changes in your brain linked to increased happiness (Curry et al., 2022).

The previous principle was about looking for the good in every day. My ultimate principle is: Strive to be the good in another person's day. When you achieve this, you become your own source of light and warmth. I thought depression was always going to be part of my life, like an addiction that I would have to fight to avoid relapsing. Then I discovered the joy of helping others. I began volunteering and looking for little ways to help those around me. When that became a key part of who I was, I truly felt like I was free of my depression and I started living a joyful life.

Sometimes I look back regretfully on the years I lost to depression. I see the opportunities I missed, like making friends or backpacking around the world instead of moldering away in bed. Most times I look back on it and see it as my phoenix moment. I died and was reborn. I did it with the help of a counsellor but without medication. I believed that medication would only treat the symptoms and not the cause of my illness. I want to emphasize that this was my choice — perhaps not the best in retrospect — and not the recommendation of a mental health professional. Medication can be helpful, especially when combined with counselling. If you are experiencing depression, I implore you to connect with a professional, whether it be your family doctor, a counsellor, or a distress line, to learn about resources and options for treatment. If you are in Canada, you can connect with Talk Suicide Canada (call 1.833.456.4566 or text 45645. Note Canada will be getting a 3-digit phone number for suicide prevention on November 30, 2023). If you are in the United States, you can dial 988 to connect with the 988 Suicide & Crisis Lifeline.

Works Cited

Curry OS, Rowland LA, Van Lissa CJ, Zlotowitz S, McAlaney J, Whitehouse H. Happy to help? A systematic review and meta-analysis of the effects of performing acts of kindness on the well-being of the actor. J Exp Soc Psychol. 2018;76:320–9.

Neff KD. Self-Compassion: Theory, Method, Research, and Intervention. Annu Rev Psychol. 2023 Jan 18;74:193-218.

Zimmerman M, Becker L. Psychiatric patients who do not believe they deserve to get better. *J Clin Psychiatry*. 2022;83(4):21br14314.

~ About Meaghan Tanaka ~

Meaghan Tanaka hails from Toronto, Canada. She works part-time as a crisis counsellor and leadership trainer, but she is proud to call herself a full-time "Homemaker" for her two young children, charming husband, and mischievous dog.

She currently struggles to find time to pursue her personal interests, but dreams of being a professional artist or eater. A few of her favorite things include spicy food, hot showers, and going down rabbit holes on Wikipedia. She is passionate about helping others through small acts of kindness.

One day, Meaghan would love to create a safe online space for people to share their stories about mental health struggles and recovery. She is always open to connecting and can be reached at meaghantanaka@gmail.com. (Just make sure to get the spelling correct).

The Positive Drip and Onyx Expressions Publishing, LLC

Presents

RELENTLESS

EMPOWERING STORIES OF OVERCOMING ADVERSITY

MY CHAPTER
"MY HARDEST BATTLE, MY UNSEEN BLESSING"

TONY LYNCH
Contributing Author

16:
My Hardest Battle, My Unseen Blessing

By Tony Lynch

Finding purpose after the loss of my son

For three days, I watched my son, Jake, fight for his life. Prior to this, I was really enjoying life with my son, but all of that changed on October 31, 2015. It was the scariest time of my life. He suffered a massive overdose. I'm sure you are thinking he was dealing with a drug addiction problem, but that wasn't the case at all. In fact, this overdose was not due to his own wrongdoing at all. The pharmacist mixed his medications wrong and caused this overdose. Jake was just seven years-old. Of course, I prayed and prayed for his speedy recovery.

Over those three days when I was praying for Jake's recovery, I reminisced about the day he was born, December 18, 2008. It was the happiest day of my life! For once in my life, everything was good. Unfortunately, things did not work out between his mother and me. We had a terrible breakup that resulted in an ugly, extensive court battle in order for me to be in my son's life. When everything finally worked out, I was thrilled. For the next few years, it was just me and my *Bubba* growing up, learning, and exploring this world together. I learned how to be a man and a father to my son.

Thankfully, through a lot of faith and prayer, he woke up. We were truly blessed! Needless to say, I breathed a sigh of relief. I was incredibly grateful that Jake survived this traumatic medical crisis and was overjoyed that this nightmarish time of our life was finally behind us.

I wish this was the end of this living nightmare, but it wasn't. For the next nine months, everything seemed normal. Jake went back to living a normal kid's life. Jake was growing up and getting just doing kid stuff. He was involved in hip hop class and rock climbing. Then, on June 14th, after a day and evening of playing and swimming with his friends, Jake went to sleep as usual, like any other healthy kid. It seemed like any other normal night. But, that all changed the next day when he woke up. He was sick and not feeling well. Like most parents, I figured it was no big deal. Unfortunately, this was not the case. Jake progressively got worse. He had a fever, was throwing up, and couldn't keep food down. This progressed over the next day and his mom decided to take him to the family doctor. The doctor immediately sent him to the emergency room. He was seen and shortly thereafter, we were airlifted to a children's hospital. A couple of hours later, during an emergency procedure, he passed of unknown causes. Needless to say, that day changed me.

I found myself in a space of uncertainty, loneliness, and darkness. I began isolating myself. I lost everything. I was alone and felt helpless and hopeless. I became homeless, and to top it off, my mother passed away. Of course, this sent me deeper down the rabbit hole of depression and hopelessness. In my mind, I had nothing to live for.

Out of desperation, I eventually began to plan my suicide, and it seemed like a good idea to "just be done with this." After 2 months of planning, I was ready. I had the whole weekend to myself; one day to come to terms, one day to enjoy some fishing, and one day to *do the do*. Yes, I was ready and had a whole plan.

When I was getting ready to execute my plan, I was interrupted by a voice that called my name. It was clear as day for me. Not only did the voice call my name, it simply said, "I love you." I'm not sure why, but hearing those words changed everything for me. After sitting there for some time, I began to make my way back home. During that journey, I was reminded of the feelings of compassion, empathy, happiness, sadness, and love. These were all the emotions and feelings I experienced when my son was alive. Having Jake in my life gave me so many wonderful memories. As I reflected on those memories, I knew I needed help to deal with the pain I was carrying. I decided to get some help.

After seeking help, I realized how little help was out there for men who were experiencing loss. I was looking for a support group, but sadly, I didn't really find any. This led me to begin a mission of connecting with other men, who, like myself, were dealing with grief. Since I couldn't find a support group, I got the idea to start one. So, I pursued this idea and started a non-profit, *MEMORIES OF US LTD*... a grief support group for men. The purpose of the group was to create a space for men to talk and be heard. For the last 3 years, I've pursued this vision. Through all of the tragedy, trauma, and homelessness I experienced, I found my purpose. My purpose in this world is to serve others by helping them to resolve their grief. I have expanded my reach through podcasting and know that I am making a positive difference.

As I mentioned, words matter. Hearing the words, "I love you," saved my life. While the loss of Jake and my mother changed the course of my life, I'm grateful that I can now see the blessing I received as well as the blessing I have become. Through my deepest pain, I discovered that I am destined to change someone's life by helping them abandon a desperate plan to die by suicide. There is power in words and even more power in fond memories. If you or someone you know is experiencing profound sadness or depression due to loss or grief, please connect with me.

~ About Tony Lynch ~

Tony Lynch is a Grief Coach, Recovery Coach, Mental Health First Aider, and Certified Suicide Prevention Coach. Following the untimely death of his parents and only son, Tony turned his pain into purpose and began providing grief support services to men all over the globe. As the founder of the non-profit organization, *Memories of Us LTD*, the *Global Grief Network*, and the *Let's Talk About It* podcast, Tony is the host of the Annual Global Grief Conference.

Tony enjoys fishing, podcasting, reading, writing, and serving others. He resides in Loveland, Colorado.

The Positive Drip and Onyx Expressions Publishing, LLC
Presents
RELENTLESS
EMPOWERING STORIES OF
OVERCOMING ADVERSITY
MY CHAPTER
"PERSISTENTLY DETERMINED"
SID OWSLEY
Contributing Author

17: Persistently Determined

BY SID OWSLEY

My own updated story of continuing to use my mantra, the 3-D's to success; Determination Determines Destination can be seen in the present moment that I am in right now. As I write these words, for the past several months I've been dealing with a situation where the career I chose and the living situation that I had created have changed dramatically and in a way that I did not expect and did not like.

In 2021, I finally achieved my dream I had been working on for a few years. I moved to Rio de Janeiro, Brazil. This move was something I wanted for a long time. I found a career that enabled me to work remotely and begin creating the lifestyle I had been planning, visualizing, dreaming about, and working toward for many years. I did not hesitate to jump on this opportunity when it afforded itself. This was not a spur-of-the-moment kind of move though. I only needed the means to create income to put my plan into action.

Years ago, I learned that if you want something bad enough, you have to be willing to create a plan and then implement it. I'm sure you've heard the old saying, "Failure to plan is a plan to fail." Well, the best way to create that plan is to find someone who is already successfully doing what you want to do. I found such a person, and it gets even better. He was not only doing what I wanted to do, he was living in the exact place I wanted to live...Brazil.

I was serious about my business and what I wanted to achieve. So, I set my plan and got busy. At that particular time, I didn't know exactly how I was going to do it, but I did know exactly what I wanted. It wasn't easy, but I did it. I took all of the necessary steps: studying, taking the exam, getting certified, and getting the necessary licenses. In the course of about two months, I was able to transition from the career I was in to this new career.

One of the things that we have to realize when we make plans is that a plan is just a framework. It is something that cannot be set totally in stone. It has to be flexible, able to be changed, and adjusted as necessary. One thing I'm sure you already know is that oftentimes, in life, there are no straight lines. The road to success is often curvy and off the beaten path. In other words, we have to recognize and understand from the very beginning that we have to be willing and able to adjust and modify the plan when we encounter obstacles and setbacks. More importantly, we have to develop a mindset that will allow us to use those detours and challenges as opportunities. As they say, we must learn to use our setbacks as setups for our comebacks. Just because things don't go as we initially planned, doesn't mean that they won't happen. It just means we may to take a different road.

So, one night while I was sitting in the living room of my cousin's house in Atlanta, Georgia, preparing for my flight to leave the next day for Rio de Janeiro, I found out that a very important part of my plan had to be modified. The person who was going to help me get situated, unexpectedly died from Covid! He was going to mentor me and help streamline the process of relocating by showing me how to get a visa to live in Brazil and how to start a business there. I had an ironclad blueprint, and he was a major piece of the plan for this new chapter of my life. Now, he wouldn't be there to help me. I had to decide if I was going to delay my trip or if I was going to continue anyway with my plans. Talk about a detour!

I decided to contact another American friend of mine, also living in Rio de Janeiro. She also knew the person that died and was just as surprised and devastated by his death as I was. I explained to her that our friend was going to help me get an apartment and asked her if she could help me. As a foreigner, you need to have the equivalent of a cosigner as well as certain documents in order to rent an apartment long-term. Things were a little more difficult than I thought it would be. As I mentioned earlier, there are no straight lines in nature and so my plan for renting an apartment did not go exactly as I planned. I found out from one of the landlords where I applied for an apartment, that one of my important documents had been suspended. I was completely confused and could not figure out why. I had this particular document for almost 20 years since I first started going to Brazil and never really had any problems with it. Then another problem crept up. I got a work assignment that was way too advanced for me since I was new to the field. Ultimately, I simply had to resign myself to getting what I could from it and beefing up my resume, but I had to let the assignment go.

I understood that just because you make a plan, doesn't mean everything is going to go exactly as you have planned and that you need to adjust and be willing to be flexible. So, with the apartment situation not working out as I planned, and the assignment ending sooner than I thought, I headed back to the United States. I was determined to get back to Brazil though. I had to find out what the problem with the document.

Upon arriving back in Brazil, I had to deal with the matter of finding out why my document had been suspended even though I never used it. This proved to be much harder than I thought it would be. It took several months to find this out and so my plan to rent an apartment during the low season was not achieved. I was not able to rectify the situation with the document until the late part of November.

Over the next year, my fiancé and I made a life for ourselves in Brazil. We moved into a condo and continued with the business of settling in and creating a life for ourselves. I had found a work assignment that was a little more steady and so I wasn't having to run back-and-forth to the United States. Things were going very well career-wise and my friend and his daughter back in the United States were preparing to move to go back to Africa so they were packing up things in the apartment and I was on the timeline that I had established a year earlier to make the final phase of my move to Brazil. So, I made a trip back to the United States to make the final move and close out my apartment there, sell my car, bring the rest of my possessions to Brazil, and see my friend and his daughter off to go back to Africa.

Things were going well over the next several months, and then things began to change in my career. The work load began to slow down and new assignments seemed to be harder to get. For several months, I worked a few more work assignments, but they were very short-term. Income was not steady and then everything seemed to slow down even more and the remote work became harder to get.

I had to make the decision to come back to the United States with very little money and had no place to stay. I continued to work on getting my career and income situation better. It was with the help of family and friends I was able to fly back to United States, stay with a friend for several weeks to begin changing my career, and getting my life back together. This was the most unfamiliar, and frankly, scary situation I've dealt with since making the move to Brazil. I did not have an established home and did not have any income coming in. I had to stay with friends, borrow some money from relatives to get an Airbnb, and I'm doing housesitting in order to keep a roof over my head while I study for my new career and create another life for myself and to return to Brazil. For me, this has been a true test of my life motto; the 3-D success plan... Determination Determines Destination. I have been truly blessed to have the help of family and friends and to have events happen that seem like miracles in order for me to continue to pursue my goals and dreams. Through my network of family and friends, I have been able to keep a roof over my head and still have the love of people who care about me. Thankfully, I have also been able to see my mother while in the United States and, most importantly, I have always been able to visit her every year on her birthday.

So, when I speak of the 3D's of success; Determination Determines Destination, I speak from a deep understanding based on my personal experience. As I mentioned before, I don't always like the way things are unfolding at the time, but ultimately, I know everything will work out because it always has worked out for me. I've learned to reframe seemingly impossible situations and turn them into opportunities. When looking at these challenges through a lens of a positive light, I seek solutions and don't get stifled by the problems at hand. I constantly remind myself that Determination Determines Destination.

I've had the opportunity to really look inward and understand how truly blessed I really am. Given all that I've been through and overcome because of the generosity and kindness of friends and family, I continue to keep the attitude of positivity. I am willing to go out of my way to help others in their hour of need, even during my time of need. I have learned to become an even stronger swimmer in the middle of the storm. No matter how ugly it may get, I know that this situation too will pass. I choose to use my obstacles to help me grow and use them to help me get better, stronger, more focused, and grateful. My goals in life have not changed, just an adjustment to the plan of how to achieve them. This is the reality of life. We cannot control the situations that happen to us, but we can control how we respond to them. By showing gratitude, love, and trust that we will overcome all obstacles and challenges we face in life. We must be assured and trust ourselves so that we will succeed beyond what we have even thought we could do. Yes, Determination Determines Destination, be ***Persistently Determined***!

~ About Sid Owsley ~

Sid Owsley is a former U.S. Marine and a former Deputy Sheriff. He holds a Bachelor's Degree in Homeland Security and Emergency Management. As a certified *Les Brown Power Voice Speaker*, Sid was one of the featured speakers in the Les Brown Power Voice Speaker Summit. Mr. Owsley has several certifications in Digital Marketing and owns Kudujuce Digital Marketing Agency.

As a Certified BlockChain Professional (CBCP), Mr. Owsley believes in being at the forefront of trends and technology as well as helping companies learn about the benefits of implementing blockchain technology. Mr. Owsley is also the host\ of the **Determination Determines Destination** podcast and has been a guest on several podcasts. Sid enjoys traveling, reading, working out, and sharing a good meal with friends.

The Positive Drip and Onyx Expressions Publishing, LLC

Presents

RELENTLESS

EMPOWERING STORIES OF OVERCOMING ADVERSITY

MY CHAPTER
"BUILDING RESILIENCE IN THE FACE OF ADVERSITY"

BENITHA SAMUEL
Contributing Author

18:
Building Resilience in the Face of Adversity

By Benitha Samuel

As the world looked on, a lot was going wrong. Maybe it was just me thinking something was wrong. Anyway, what do you expect from someone who has no hope, no courage, no drive, or desire to live? That was my case as a child.

I had invested all my love in my mother. I believed in everything she promised me, but life happened, and took my mother away from me. Taking away my mother, took away my desire to live, learn, and strive for anything in life. As a child, I always looked at myself in the mirror, and told myself 'you're going to be an amazing broadcaster who will work for BBC, and CNN and achieve greatness.' I had confidence in myself and with my mother by my side, I believed I could conquer the world. My confidence was shattered when she passed on. My positive beliefs died with her.

I kept building a negative wall around me that allowed no positivity. It was one traumatic childhood experience. I even tried committing suicide, but God spared my life. So, just like most growing children, I lived on and did as I was asked.

I was just swimming through life, but lacked direction. Sometimes, I felt like I was drowning rather than swimming. My first break came when I left home to stay with my aunt. A lot started changing, and that was the beginning of a new me. I was always a lone walker, different from other children. I grew up in a family that had no idea what encouraging a child meant. We were not fortunate to have someone in the family cheer us on by telling us we were strong enough or capable of achieving anything great in life. Left to our own devices, we could only imagine that we could be great from the movies we watched and the books we read.

I would read, sing, and act to console myself because every event around me felt like I was being mocked and looked down on. Accepting one's loss and finding the courage to live again takes time even for an adult, much less for a child that has no grip on life yet. Staying with my aunt gave me a chance to witness a different world.

I was determined to take what I learned while staying with my aunt with me as I embarked on my higher education journey.

Although my father wanted me to become a lawyer, I chose to study Communication Art. I was quiet, lonely, and withdrawn, yet eager to study so I could be seen in life. I had a desire, but I lacked confidence. Thankfully, even though I saw no potential or greatness in me, others believed in me. For a while, I had to settle on borrowing their belief in me.

I became involved with the church at the university and began to grow my confidence as I took on several roles. My first position was as a Prayer Coordinator in the youth department. I was later selected as a Vice

President of the youth department and when I got to my final year; I became the Sisters' Coordinator of the church. Being a Sisters' Coordinator required that I managed the sister's fellowship, spoke to sisters directly, teaching, advising, praying with them, and organizing programs for them. The position gave me the chance to do things I never believed I could. I began to flourish. In fact, I remember staring into my mirror, and for the first time, telling myself that I was capable of anything in life - and actually believing it.

Today, I am still grateful for that experience because it was the best beginning anyone like me could have. I am grateful that people saw me and gave me a chance. I believe that God put me in a position where I could not reject these chances. It was the first step and from that point; I have never stopped desiring to take on more. That was why when the time to go for service (a compulsory 1-year service to the country), I made a decision to stay wherever I would be posted after the 1-year service.

I ended up in Kano State, one of the Northern states in my country Nigeria, to serve my motherland. To earn a living in this strange place, every Saturday I would go out to weddings, snap pictures, go to the lab, print the photos and then sell them to the guests. I did this for nearly eight months. I struggled to put food on my table in a strange land where my father had bluntly told me I was on my own because I disobeyed him by staying there.

After I served as planned, I decided to continue living there. I chose to stay for two reasons. Firstly, I felt like coming back home would be like returning to a comfort zone I was desperately trying to escape. Secondly, I knew I would not be able to relate with others in the home. I needed outside communication if I was ever going to overcome my childhood experience and strive for more. So, I had to decide.

In the process of stretching to find my true identity, I learned a lot and I would like to share some of what I learned with you. Self-acceptance, self-forgiveness, self-inspiration/celebration, and the importance of self-development are four factors I believe played a huge role in my healing process. I trust these concepts may help you as well regarding whatever adversity you may be facing.

SELF-ACCEPTANCE helped me realize that whoever God created, He created with a purpose and that what we go through in life is all part of what makes us who we are. I realized that acceptance is very important to anyone interested in growing. This was my first lesson. As I understood the power of acceptance, a lot changed. I remember an incident during my university days as the Vice President of the youth department in my church. A sister spoke to me about what she was going through. It was what I had gone through and allowed me to be confident while assuring her it was not the end of life. I told her to look at me, and told her if I could make it to that point, she definitely could. After that discussion, when I sat on my bed, looking at myself in my mind's mirror, I told myself, "This is just what God wanted you to do with all that you have been through; use it positively."

From that moment, my inner healing began. I learned to accept that everything I went through was a scar that must be seen for the glory of God. I accepted it and forgave myself for feeling sorry for myself and my circumstances.

I missed a lot of opportunities because I was so soaked in my grief and forgot to live. I hated people and never believed in their sincere love and care. I hated myself for still being alive after mum's death. But as I began to understand the power of self-forgiveness, I could feel my peace return.

I realized I had to let go of the past and move on. Now that I've done that, I feel much happier.

FORGIVENESS helped me get back my power and authority over negativity. It also helped hasten my inner healing and guided my focus away from regrets and guilt, and toward gratitude. As I was going through the forgiveness stage, I became my own inspirator. I told myself that I could face my fears, step out there, and demand what is mine. I started verbalizing positive affirmations, and it worked! I suggest you try practicing this. I know from experience; it feels beautiful when you tell yourself you can do a thing and you become your number one fan. I have experienced the power of SELF-**INSPIRATION.** Also, because I knew what had been through and the sacrifices I had made, I began to celebrate my little wins. This made a huge difference for me. I encourage you to do the same.

SELF-CELEBRATION will help you understand how to listen to your inner voice. When the voices of others cheering you on fade, your voice will be the only voice still cheering you on... hear it, believe it, live it, use it to do even more.

The last one I want to share here is **SELF-DEVELOPMENT**. When you take time to celebrate your little wins, you will naturally feel like you can do more and be better than where you are at that time. I used to say: I had to take the first step to train myself on how to work with a camera. I had to sacrifice my time and energy to study editing. I had to spend money on data to learn and improve my skills. Now I've learned to say I got a chance to... It is the same for anyone that wants to be better, seen, heard, and recognized in this world. I encourage you to look at those obstacles you face as opportunities you can use to grow and evolve.

Now, I gladly share these lessons on global stages as a victor who is no longer the victim. I teach people about the power of acceptance because that is the first step that helped me forgive myself, wake up to the call of purpose, and find peace in the process. I have fallen in love with teaching these lessons to the youth and women around the world. I am now passionate about helping them discover their true identity and uniqueness, and build thought patterns that make them the priority of their lives. I gladly hold their hands as they transition from negative beliefs and embrace living a life of positivity.

I am now a voice! It is no longer a surprise to me that God loves me because he has always been with me. Trust me, God is always in the picture, no matter what. Don't give up on yourself because of what is happening around you. Be resilient and relentless in all situations and God will make all things beautiful in His time, just as He has done for me.

~ About Benitha Samuel ~

BENITHA SAMUEL is a positive self-thought influencer interested in helping others find, build, and express positive self-thought, speak, and lead confidently. She is a self-love, acceptance, forgiveness, celebration, and development advocate. Benitha is a voice on a mission and is God's masterpiece.

With her knowledge and daily experiences in building a positive mindset/self-thought, she is passionate about helping youths discover their true identity and uniqueness, build a thought pattern that makes them a priority, while speaking and leading with confidence. She believes she can work with you to break repeated negative self-thought patterns, daily self-rejection, constant acceptance of negative opinions, and lack of confidence in your personal vision and purpose.

Her story has always been about the adverse events in her life until she discovered that she was actually the writer and actor of those negative scripts and that it was time to flip to HER NEXT CHAPTER where she is now the heroine. As such, she now has not only built a thought pattern that helps her stay positive, but has begun to help others build a thought pattern that makes them a priority.

Benitha is the founder of THE BENNY EXPRESSION, host of The Benny Expression Show (#tbexshow), host of the Voice on a Mission podcast, and Lead Coach at BENNY SPEAKERS ACADEMY. An author, mindset, self-thought influencer, global speaker, educationist, and host of PPS SCOOP; a primary school podcast where she hosts students and parents to boost their confidence and communication skills. As a lover of God and a global speaker, Benitha has spoken on many stages, both physical and virtual, as well as hosted speakers around the world on mindset, self-acceptance, self-thoughts, and self-love-related topics on her show (#tbexshow).

She loves to sing, write, dance, act, network, and speak

Her mission is to impact one person at a time whose testimony will impact the next person, and her vision is to see people look at themselves with faith and love for who they are.

Her personal and favorite quote is; "YOU ARE ENOUGH AND MORE PLUS" Benny Expression

The Positive Drip and Onyx Expressions Publishing, LLC
Presents

RELENTLESS

EMPOWERING STORIES OF OVERCOMING ADVERSITY

MY CHAPTER
"IT'S ALL ABOUT PERSEPECTIVE"

31

NIT SUA
Contributing Author

19:
It's All About Perspective
By Nit Sua

In order to remind us of our *personal greatness*, Coach "Dee" would frequently use these commanding words during basketball practice ... "Give yourselves a clap !!!" ... and ... in response, the entire team would provide one loud thunderous clap in unison.

Seconds ago, this Canadian Gymnasium was Chaotic & filled with Escalating Excitement!!! - It's Sunday April 23, 2023 and I'm standing at the left elbow of our foul line, hunched over at the waist with my hands on my thighs, breathing intensely. There are less than seven seconds left in the 3rd quarter of the last basketball game of my very first "Boys - (Under 13 years old) - Rep Basketball Team" season. As the referee blew the whistle, I swiftly cut diagonally across the key to lose my defender and receive the in bounds pass from my teammate who was situated underneath our basket. As the ball entered into my hands, I glanced up at the game clock and saw that there was only 6.3 seconds left in this 3rd quarter. I knew that I had to move fast, so I speedily dribbled like a flash of light towards the opposition's basket as my teammates cleared a narrow pathway for me to squeeze through. Within a blink of an eye, I reached the opposition's foul line and began my lay up, I then gathered the ball, and before I knew it, I was airborne and in "mid flight" as I released my shot ...

... But ... before I tell you how this story unfolds, let me bring you back to Saturday, August 27, 2022. It was 10 a.m., and I had just entered a huge college athletic centre escorted by my uncle, who is also my godfather. There were 12 to 13-year-old boys everywhere filling the hallways, but all that mattered to me was the whereabouts of Court #2. This is where I had to register and state that I was present for the 11 a.m. Basketball Team tryout. Out of 62 attending boys, 20 of them would be invited back to the second tryout 24 hours later. Gratefully, I was one of them. This was the beginning of my quest to make a Rep Basketball team. Many more tryouts, with other teams, followed within the remaining month of September 2022 and along with these tryouts, came offers to join some of those teams. However, there was a specific team that I had secretly hoped would reach out to me, but the deadline for choosing and committing to the "other" teams was soon approaching. Due to the uncertainty, and my yearning desire to play Rep Basketball, I had to decide quickly amongst my other choices because *"THE"* e'mail that I was waiting for didn't arrive. However, "just" as I was about to select a team to commit to, I received the e'mail that I was hoping, wishing, and praying for and I happily replied "Yes!!!" to the invitation to join their squad. It felt like I had won the Lottery!!! I was now a member of the "TN" - (Under 13 Boys) - Rep Basketball Team. My head coach, Coach "Dee", is a strong, passionate, stern, loving man who believes in the importance of creating "protectors" who display drive, passion, commitment, hard work, heart, aggression, and precision. Coach "Dee" demanded *excellence*, not *perfection*, from all of his players, and I was excitedly up for the challenge. I now had eleven new brothers and to see my last name on the back of *my* very own basketball jersey, alongside my favourite number, which was #31, was a dream come true.

Before today's final game, we had 3 tryout dates, 83 full team practices, 3 social family team get-togethers, and a twelve-game basketball season. Our record was twelve losses and zero wins. In my mind, we were on route to peaking at the right time. According to my *the glass is always half full perspective,* these first twelve games were a way to work on, build on, and polish up our overall game performances so we would be ready for the most important game of our season: the "FIRST" of three games at the Under 13 Boys Basketball Championships in April 2023.

The results of Game 1 were : Team "TN", which was "us" = 30 pts & Team NBD = 48 pts - Although we lost, it was ok because we still had two more games left to play.

The results of Game 2 were : Team "TN" = 48 pts & Team PP = 57 pts - Yes, we lost again.

… and last but not least …

The results of Game 3 were : Team "TN" = 37 pts & Team DKD = 52 pts.

At this point in time we had a record of Fifteen Losses and a Whopping Zero Wins

The stage was now set for the final game of our entire basketball season, which was on Sunday, April 23, 2023 @ 9 am against Team "MM"

… As I was soaring through the air, you could hear a pin drop in this once roaring gymnasium. As everything flashed before my eyes, I couldn't help but remember the many life shaping lessons that I had learned along the way ever since the very beginning of our season … and … here are some of them:

Coach "Dee" taught us ...

1. **It's not what happens to you, it's how you handle it.** For example, it's important not to get down on yourself when you miss a shot. Stay positive, give yourself a clap, come back on defense, and go after it again.

2. **To *ALWAYS* believe in yourself no matter what - and - that we HAVE** the skills to play basketball & that we "Belong" in this division amongst our peers.

3. **To Follow our Dreams & Visualize** ourselves succeeding - It's been proven that those who actively visualize shooting & scoring in basketball are just as successful as those who physically practiced, shot, and scored.

4. **To always enjoy ourselves along the way.** As my coaches have always told us, it's a "process" and it's important to make sure that you always enjoy the process.

5. **To Never give up!!!** - and - that our "**Effort**" is the one variable that we can always control.

6. **To always put yourself in a position to succeed first.** For example, we must completely learn and understand the offensive and defensive plays that our coaches have been repetitively teaching us so that we'll be able to perform properly in games and specific situations.

7. That **practicing correctly leads to correct outcomes**. For example, my coach taught me, and us, the importance of how and when to use a bounce pass, of how and when to pass fake, and why we never ride along our guarded player's hip while defending against him. When it comes to shooting, I learned that I must put an arc on my shot so it has a chance of falling into the basket. Last, but not least, I learned the importance of quickly recognizing an opportunity and taking advantage of it

immediately before the opportunity closes, like when attacking a gap in the opposing team's defense in order to score.

8. About the importance of being a **good, coachable teammate and friend.** Regardless of having twelve losses & zero wins, we still like each other. We hang out and chat with one another in between games, we high five and encourage each other while on the basketball court, we have memorable silly lunches together on multiple-game days, and last but not least, we also laugh amongst one another.

9. To always **learn from our mistakes.** Mistakes are meant to be learned from so we can adjust and execute properly the next time and forever.

10. To always **be brave and aggressive** in the moment. The very first lesson that I remember Coach "Dee" teaching us was the importance of being and staying aggressive while on the court and that we would never get into trouble for being aggressive when it came to playing offense, defense, pressing, cutting, rebounding, and most of all attacking the opponent's basket to score.

11. To Always play to **support your teammates unselfishly.** I believed in this. I believed that if you played for your teammates unselfishly, they would be there for you just as you are for them every single time.

As my flashback drew to a close, I was still in "mid-flight" and my eyes were intensely focused on the basket as I released my shot.

The ball looped over the basket's rim, hit the square on the backboard softly, and then went into the basket. I had scored a buzzer beater with 1.8 seconds left on the game clock and the crowd erupted in a frenzy of clapping, cheering, and bell clanging !!! The score was now : Team "TN" = 51 pts & Team "MM" = 36 pts.

As the 3rd quarter's game clock struck zero and the buzzer sounded, the five of us excitedly rushed to our teams' bench where we were greeted by our awaiting high-fiving teammates & smiling coaches.

We played out the remaining eight minutes of the 4th, and final, quarter and celebrated regardless of the score. Our mission had been accomplished. We went from being twelve strangers in August 2022 to becoming a band of brothers by the end of our 2023 Basketball Championships experience on April 23, 2023. I am so grateful to my teammates for making my rookie Rep Basketball season exciting, entertaining, and memorable. I realize that this is the beginning of something special for me in my life, and I cannot wait to see what unfolds for me next as I continue to strive for *"excellence,* not *perfection,"* in my remaining days.

Before I end my chapter, I would like to thank my amazing Head Coach, Coach "Dee", for taking a chance on me, and the Assistant Coach, Mr. J.T, and the Team Manager, Mr. A. S., for providing me, and the rest of us, with a positive, encouraging, and inspiring environment to grow as basketball players and young men.

... and ...

Last but not least, I would like to thank my parents for investing their hard-earned dollars, irreplaceable time, and undying belief in me so I could turn my Rep Basketball dreams into a Reality. I love you very, very, much Mom and Dad !!!

For those of you who enjoyed my chapter, please remember to be **Brave, Aggressive, and Coachable** during those important moments in life where you find yourselves going after the things that you want on route to stepping into the greatest version of yourselves. Ladies & gentlemen, friends & family, give yourselves a clap!!! -

Sincerely,

Nit Sua

... Ps - Just in case you're wondering, the final score of our very last game of the 2023 basketball season was Team "TN" = 72 pts & Team "MM" = 49 pts - Our record was now Fifteen Losses & "One" Amazing & Unforgettable Win !!! - Look out world, here "We" come!!!

~ About Nit Sua ~

I AM ...

- I am Original
- I am Ambitious
- I am Passionate
- I am Athletic
- I am Educated
- I am Artistic
- I am Curious
- I am Attentive
- I am Upbeat
- I am Creative
- I am Intelligent
- I am Skilled
- I am Loving
- I am Strong
- I am Generous
- I am Incredible
- I am Loyal
- I am Competitive
- I am Unselfish
- I am Caring
- I am Co-operative
- I am Understanding
- I am Knowledgeable
- I am Friendly

... and ...

- I am Kind

... I AM "Nit Sua"

#GloryToGod

The Positive Drip and Onyx Expressions Publishing, LLC
Presents
RELENTLESS
EMPOWERING STORIES OF
OVERCOMING ADVERSITY
MY CHAPTER
"SPEAKING OF LOVE"
LA TOYA BOND
Contributing Author

20:
Speaking of Love
By La Toya Bond

My father was an amazing guy. He had an infectious laugh, and his spirit was magnetic. He was the type of guy who made everybody feel like somebody special. If you were to place him in a crowded room of 100 people, he would be the smartest person in the entire room. My dad was an award-winning radio / tv broadcast engineer for many years. My dad had a deep understanding of the emotion we call love, and he often expressed his love through the lyrics of legendary Motown music. His favorite singer was Eddie Kendrix. Born and raised in the city of Detroit, he was one of the first in his family to go to college. While attending Wayne State University, he developed a lifelong love affair with the game of basketball. He was the shortest point guard on the team, but he could slam dunk the basketball with either hand. By all outward appearances, my dad lived a rewarding life. But there were parts of him that were only known to him. Eventually, his private struggles became public.

On March 2, 2020, I woke up in the middle of the night. I looked at my phone and noticed that I had several missed calls and text messages from family members. I soon discovered that my dad had taken his own life in a murder-suicide. Reportedly, he shot and killed his wife moments before turning the gun on himself. He later died from an apparent self-inflicted gunshot wound. The murder-suicide took place inside of the couple's home. They had only been married for 9 months. **When he died, a part of me died too.**

In the beginning, I had a wide range of emotions. Everyone experiences grief and loss in a different way. My first reaction was shock and extreme sadness. It all seemed surreal, like being in the middle of a dream. I was broken, and I found it hard to breathe. As with most suicide loss survivors, I was also angry with my dad. It was hard to comprehend the fact that he was capable of such a life-altering act. I felt a deep sense of sadness about the fact that I was not there to help him on that fateful night. I often wonder if I had been there, would the outcome be the same? I am his daughter, and had no idea that he was in so much pain. I was not aware that he was struggling mentally. How could I be so blind? This is the worst thing that could ever happen to anyone — **MURDER-SUICIDE!** His actions devastated the hearts of many, especially those who loved him and his wife.

My dad's memorial ceremony took place in Detroit, Michigan, on March 15, 2020, just a few days before the Covid-19 pandemic. This is when my grieving process began. The country went into lockdown, and we all were forced to limit our access to the world. I felt robbed of my life, my freedom, and most of all, my dad. I soon began displaying feelings of extreme sadness. My sleep patterns changed dramatically. I started experiencing night terrors where I would envision my dad's last moments on Earth. I was at my lowest point and in excruciating mental pain.

Then one day, I hit rock bottom. I was sitting in my kitchen, when suddenly, I started to feel extremely dizzy. I could not hold my head up straight, and walking was nearly impossible. I had never experienced any form of illness in my entire life. I had to be driven to the hospital, where a series of tests were performed. The doctors suspected that I might have suffered a mild stroke. I was admitted into the hospital. However, after three days of testing, it was determined that I did not have a stroke, but my blood pressure was extremely high. They would not release me until my blood pressure was regulated.

During my 3rd night in the hospital, I cried out to God. I felt so alone and afraid. Losing a loved one to suicide is a lonely journey, especially when it is a murder-suicide. It is a heart-wrenching experience which can also be confusing. It usually comes with a lot of mixed-up feelings, including anger and guilt. I was experiencing such a wide range of emotions that I grew concerned about my thoughts and feelings. I asked GOD to help me because I did not want to meet the same fate as my dad. I realized, in that moment, that I had to make some changes in the way I was handling my grief.

My dad was a very important person in my life. I valued him and I cherished the love he had for me. I needed to find a better way to cope with my loss. I needed to give my pain a greater purpose. It is not possible to ever let go of someone you've lost to suicide; yet it is possible to go forward and live a quality life. This is exactly what I have done.

After my release from the hospital, I went home and began to channel my inner creativity. I wiped the sawdust off an old jigsaw and started creating one-of-a-kind wooden art pieces. I found this to be calming and therapeutic. The adorable art pieces I made during that time will forever be sacred to me. I call them my "Therapy Pieces." I also started a cottage home bakery business. The kitchen has been my playground since I was a teenager. I feel a sense of peace when I am working in the kitchen. I love preparing soul food meals and desserts from scratch. I promoted my baked goods on social media and there was no shortage of support. On weekends, I would meet my customers at the local Walmart to sell my baked goods. The response was incredible. I was discovering new ways to manage my grief – baking and making wooden art. I was starting to feel better, but I knew I needed more.

Because my dad died in such a tragic way, I needed to find a way to honor him. I wanted my dad to be remembered for the way he lived, not the way he died. Before the tragedy, I knew very little about the subject of suicide prevention. Since the tragedy, I have become an advocate for mental health and suicide prevention. I now actively participate in suicide loss survivor support groups. I also serve on the board of directors for Kevin's Song, a non-profit organization whose mission is to educate and empower others to prevent suicide. My advocacy efforts have attracted the attention of several media publications. I have traveled great distances as a keynote speaker for suicide prevention conferences. My greatest hope is to create a world where suicide no longer exists.

Early in his career, my dad hosted an award-winning radio show, "**Speaking of Sports**." To honor him, I created a podcast, "**Speaking of Love**" as a platform for spreading love. "Speaking of Love" aims to serve individuals like my dad who are struggling with the effects of mental health challenges; which often leads to suicide. When I am hosting a podcast episode, I feel connected to my dad. It's like I am walking in his gift. He was a master in the art of radio/tv broadcasting. The podcast has positively helped me cope with my grief. I am eternally grateful for all the guests who have appeared on my podcast. Those 120+ individuals from all around the world are the people who enhanced my life during this difficult stage of grief. This work has been incredibly life changing.

What I learned about myself during this experience is that I am a strong woman. I have struggled with low self-esteem for many years. But losing my dad so tragically has taught me that I am, indeed, strong. I also learned that I am a woman who is determined to impact the world. I used to be afraid to share my voice, but now I speak loud about what matters to me the most, like suicide prevention. I have learned that my voice has value. I believe the world needs more love, and I was born to be the love that the world needs.

Based on my personal experience and knowledge, here are five techniques that can help you cope with losing someone to suicide:

Educate yourself about suicide and its causes. This education will help you along your journey of healing. Prior to my dad's passing, I knew very little about the subject of suicide. I have learned that suicide is a mental health crisis, and it does not discriminate. It can happen to anyone.

Being a suicide loss survivor can be a lonely journey. Please talk to someone. You will need therapy and it's okay. Facing your grief alone will make the healing process more difficult.

Do something, on a consistent basis, to honor your loved one's memory. My dad loved radio broadcasting. He was a former radio show host. As a way to honor him, I created a podcast named after his former radio show. This is one sure way to help you stay connected to your loved one through their physical absence.

Do not let your loved one die in vain. Become an advocate! Participate in walks and activities within the suicide prevention community. Be a voice for the voiceless. Turn your pain into a greater purpose.

Speaking of Love - Be an instrument of love. Open your heart to spread more love to those around you. People who feel loved are less likely to take their own lives.

At some point in our lives, we will inevitably lose someone we love. The loss of a loved one can be extremely difficult to overcome, especially when it involves a murder-suicide. Coping with life as a suicide loss survivor can become a struggle, but you can rise above your pain and live a quality life. My purpose for writing this chapter is to provide tools to help others heal after losing a loved one to suicide. Thank you for taking the time to read my chapter, **Speaking of Love,** a journey in pursuit of the strongest magnetic force on the planet Earth, Love!

~ About La Toya Bond ~

La Toya is a legal support professional, radio personality and a small business owner. She is also the host of "Speaking Of Love Podcast," created in honor of her father who took his own life in a murder-suicide. Since the tragedy, La Toya has become an advocate for mental health & suicide prevention. Her desire is to help save the lives of people who are struggling with mental health challenges, which often leads to suicide. To date, La Toya has recorded over 120 life-changing podcast episodes. She interviews people from all around the world with the sole intention of spreading love. As a minority woman, La Toya is nationally recognized by Black Women In Radio (BWIR) for her outstanding & influential contributions to Black radio culture and digital media around the globe.

Before switching career paths, La Toya worked as a school office administrator for nearly two decades. In 2017, she was awarded the *National Life Changer Of The Year Award* for positively impacting the lives of her students. La Toya is also the Executive Board Secretary for the Down Syndrome Guild of Southeast Michigan, a non-profit organization dedicated to serving children with disabilities. Additionally, she also serves on the Board of Directors for Kevin's Song, a non-profit organization dedicated to ending suicide. La Toya has been featured in several media publications for her advocacy efforts, including Fox 2 News, Macomb Daily News, The Michigan Chronicle, The Oakland Press, Authority Magazine, Detroit Praise Network, Beasley Media and more.

La Toya is a *Jane Of All Trades*. She was born and raised in Detroit Michigan. Her leadership skills were acquired at a young age as the oldest sibling in her family. She has a passion for serving humanity. She currently works as a legal support professional in her hometown, a job she truly adores. In 2018, she landed the role of "radio co-host" for a local radio program, also located in Detroit. She proudly runs a cottage bakery and wooden craft business out of her home. During her spare time, La Toya enjoys reading and collecting books and magazines. She likes to reward herself monthly with retail therapy sessions at her neighborhood TJ Maxx Store. She comes from a big family where food is the glue that strengthens her family "BOND"! She is highly sought after for her unique ability to prepare delicious soul food meals and homemade desserts – all from scratch. She is an avid lover of red lipstick and Coca-Cola Drinks.

La Toya is the mother of one adult daughter, **Crystal,** who recently graduated with honors from the University of Michigan. The apple of La Toya's eye is her beloved tuxedo cat, **Faith,** with whom she rescued from an animal shelter 13 years ago. La Toya is a respected community leader who believes that spreading love is the secret to her success.

The Positive Drip and Onyx Expressions Publishing, LLC
Presents

RELENTLESS

EMPOWERING STORIES OF OVERCOMING ADVERSITY

MY CHAPTER
WHEN "ADVERSITY" ATTACKS:
CONQUER OR CRUMBLE???

DR. NELSON BELTIJAR
Visionary Author

21: When "Adversity" Attacks: Conquer or Crumble ???

By Dr. Nelson Beltijar

Imagine this - I haven't walked, upright on my own, for almost 4 years - that's one thousand six hundred and fifty-one days to be exact - in fact, the last time I had fully used my legs was on June 26, "2016." That's right !!! - June 26th "2016" !!! - However, everything finally changed for me on January 3rd "2021." On this day, I was re-born, transformed, and ready to reclaim my place in the world, only this time armed with the sky opening epiphanies to water the seeds of the souls around me.

Ladies and Gentlemen, I'm wondering if there's anyone out there who has ever had life hand you something that you didn't expect ???

If yes, then we're kindred spirits and you'll understand, hear, and feel the following words on these upcoming pages

"Adversity" truly introduces a person to themselves. In fact, "Adversity" is a word that no earthly human being can escape while on this planet – Agreed ???

My friends, I'm the kind of guy who knows what it's like to climb that mountain of ambition and success, get to the top, enjoy the view the for a while, only to come crashing down, spiralling down, losing everything that I had ever worked for in a blink of an eye. Talk about humbling, so humbling.

I was lucky enough to build a thriving Physical Therapy Private Practice specializing in Injury Assessment, Treatment, and Rehabilitation and I'll never forget this, it was May 2016 and we were on the second floor of my studio clinic loft celebrating, Celebrating, clanging the champagne glasses - which were secretly filled with Diet Coke or Ginger Ale - CELEBRATING immensely because we had reached a monumental goal.

However, a week later, 168 hours after that joyous moment in time, I was shockingly diagnosed with cancer and immediately admitted into the hospital for supervision, evaluation, and chemotherapy treatments for the remainder of 2016.

You're not going believe this, to add salt to the wound, I even lost my ability to walk, as a secondary complication, and became a prisoner of a wheelchair for the following 3 years.

The reason I share this with you, is to remind you that "Adversity" will attack you any time it wants regardless of your age, gender, religion, or status and when it does will you find a way to Conquer it or will you Crumble beneath it ???

My "2017" wasn't any easier, it was filled with Tumour Removal Surgeries, Hospital Discharges, In-home Faintings, 911 ambulance calls, Surgical Wound Complications, Hospital Re-admissions, countless Downtown Doctor(s) appointments, Cancer Spreading False Alarms, which by the way was my favourite bump in the road, Spinal Infections, and In-Home Antibiotic IV Drip Treatments. My "2017" was nothing but a blur and a year where I couldn't catch a break.

Eventually, My 2018 rolled around and it's ironic that I'm a Physical Therapist because my entire 2018 was filled with my own physical rehabilitation "project" where the goal was to graduate from my imprisoning wheelchair of 3 years into a mobile walker, then on to "2" canes, then eventually to a single cane, with the aim of triumphantly returning back to full functional ability walking on my own alongside my friends and family once again.

My Friends, would you be brave enough to go left when every qualified person around you was leading you to the right ???

As I was forced to live in the hospitals, in 2016 & 2017, because it was no longer safe for me to stay at home, I was faced with becoming a prisoner of my own hospital bed, however, I refused to let my mind remain trapped in that hospital room. Instead, I'd let my brain roam freely beyond the four walls of my room, and the entire hospital, as I would visualize myself out in the world living a typical Monday, Tuesday, Wednesday, Thursday, Friday Saturday, and Sunday. I would mentally see, hear, and feel myself going through a typical day, it's typical errands, it's typical conversations, and it's typical arguments, with patients, friends, and family. You see, for almost 3 years, I would use the tool of mental imagery to trick my subconscious into believing that I was out in the world living instead of being stuck in the hospital bed slowly dying.

Yes, the doctors said that I was tumour-filled and it was completely unsafe for me to leave the hospital and return back into my life. However, regardless of the words that they spoke, I had already made up my mind that I was going to return back into the life that I had reluctantly left behind even if that meant I had to create my own fantasy of a reality within the confines of my mind, which I did.

It was obvious to everyone that I was stubbornly refusing to accept the picture that my Cancer doctors were painting of myself and my current health situation. As a result, I dug even deeper into my parallel universe and alternative form of reality and employed the technical conquering game skills of one of my favourite childhood pastimes.

Ladies & Gentlemen, have any of you ever played the video game called Pac Man, where the Pac Man icon eats up the dots in the video game ??? - Well, as silly as this may sound, I would visualize that I had an internal Pac Man icon within my own body whose purpose was to gobble away all of my Cancer cells. I did this every day at every single breakfast, lunch, dinner, and bedtime while living in the hospital. Crazy huh ???

As gullible as this may sound, I tapped into the power of visualization once again during the years of 2016, 2017, and 2018 and I'd mentally see myself walking, completely upright on my own, down specific streets, surrounded by specific people, walking passed specific buildings & stores, high fiving one another in celebration as we reached our symbolic finish line.

You see, I was foolish enough to believe in the impossible and I suspended my disbelief long enough to slip the principles of mental imagery and visualization into my cancer battling toolbox before doubt and skepticism had a chance to creep in.

There's a common thought that there's a mind, body, and spirit connection but to me that was just words on a page up until I totally committed to including these principles into my treatments and physical rehabilitation.

Although my professional, pre-determined, and physical hospital environment had been already established as the specific backdrop for my story to unfold, it was via the tools of mental imagery and visualization, that I was able to creatively construct my own reality and put myself in position to Win.

As difficult as all this may sound, the above text was the "easy" part of my cancer battling journey.

On top of all of this, I was forced to "live" in "5" different hospitals from June 2016 - November 2017 and my first Cancer doctor, that's right my VERY FIRST Cancer doctor, let's call him "Dr. K", gave up on me and told my family that I was terminal and that he and the hospital could do nothing else for me and that he was going to transfer me to the Palliative Care team to ensure that I would be "comfortable" and "painfree" in my remaining days. When I heard this, it was like a sword swooped downward and cut me at the knees and my life flashed before my eyes. After wallowing in self-pity for about 10 minutes I promised myself that if I was going to die, I would go out in a bang, climb one more mountain, and chase down one last purpose filled goal before my time on Earth was done regardless if adversity had grabbed hold of my ankles trying to pull me down along with it. Instead of writing my goodbye letters, I laid in my hospital bed, staring at the ceiling, tears rolling down the right side of my face, thinking, brainstorming, and dreaming of ways of how I could contribute to the lives of my younger family members. It was then that the light bulb of my mind had switched on and it became clear to me that my last undying mission was to write a blog, a blog that contained the knowledge and life nuggets that I had acquired with my short time on this planet. This blog would be my life's curtain call. You see, at that time, I had a 6-year-old nephew, a 5 and 3 year-old niece, and 2 brand newborn twins, who I loved dearly, but I also knew that I wasn't going to get a chance to see them grow up and this broke my heart. It became my yearning desire to create this blog to leave it behind for them so I could still, so I could STILL, be a part of their lives even after I had passed away.

But you want to hear something funny ??? - It looks like the joke's on me.

LET'S FAST FORWARD TO SEPTEMBER "2018" ...

1) My "NEW" team of cancer doctors at a different hospital, who fought for me and tried everything to keep me alive, miraculously stamped me cancer free on September 28th, 2018 and told me to go live my life - Yes !!!

2) That blog that I specifically created to leave behind for my "5" younger family members has ended up trickling across the planet resulting in a global readership - which was never the plan. Crazy huh ???

... and last, but, not least ...

3) A global community has accidentally evolved, and is rallying around, and currently walking alongside that blog - It's so humbling and I still can't believe it.

I don't tell you this to brag. I share this with you to show you:

- How "Adversity" introduced, and converted, me into a stronger more resilient me.

- How "Adversity" pulled me away from faltering and introduced me to the importance of having to fight.

- How "Adversity" introduced and inspired one last undying goal in me to create that love filled blog for my younger family members.

- How "Adversity" turned my mind "on" to the possibilities of what I could do in my perceived remaining days instead of turning it off.

... Instead of me lying in my hospital bed waiting for the coffin to arrive, I used my perceived remaining days to "Accidentally" create a globally impactful blog. I sincerely believe that the main reason my blog has been so well received is because I chose to invite the world into the honesty of my dark and vulnerable place allowing them to mentally sit with me. I had learned what it felt like to feel inadequate, insignificant, invisible, unheard, unseen, lost, alone, lonely, scared, and unsure. Words I never knew before, words that terrified me, and words that almost buried me and I think that it's these specific words, and my newly found feelings of Empathy, that has made my blog relatable and embraceable to the masses around the globe.

The detrimental effects of cancer on my health combined with the experienced uncertainty of my return to work put me in a very difficult and stressful situation. In a blink of an eye my everyday life, as I knew it, was taken away from me. Although I may look grinfully the same on the outside nowadays, my battle with cancer has forever changed me on the inside. As fate would have it, as a result of my physical and emotionally filled cancer battling challenges, I've evolved into a Professional Empowerment Coach who's affectionately become labeled a Resilience Expert. It's funny how we have to go through the fires of life and come out the other end victorious in order for people to want to hear what we have to say.

I'll be the first one to tell anybody that if I didn't get sick with cancer, I would've remained on my life's path of being a Physical Therapist & Clinic Owner and I would've NEVER created the www.ThePositiveDrip.com blog. Perhaps it's true what they say - "Life happens FOR you, instead of to you"

You may not agree with me and my mental imagery and visualization techniques, and yes, I'm not an expert in this psycho-motor field of science, but I'm gratefully still here, completely alive, and I've recently put a checkmark beside one of the things on my bucket list - I achieved the freedom of walking completely on my own, when I placed my cane into the closet "Forever", on January 3rd, 2021. Friends & Family are now happily asking me what's next for me and I aloofly reply - "whatever my mind can think up". Perhaps my next goal and my next metaphorical mountain to climb, will be to trot, jog, run, and / or sprint once again by December 31, 2021.

After almost being untimely ushered off of this planet, it's ironic that the greatest life lesson that I had ever learned was while I living in the 5 different hospitals in 2016 & 2017 surrounded by death and sickness 24 / 7. My travelling soul had come to the sky opening realization that the biggest lie that we've ALL been led to believe, including me, is that we all have "Time" and a long list of "Somedays" and an Unlimited amount of "I'll Do It Later" opportunities. Truth is, that's completely false. Nobody knows the day or the hour of one's last breath. My spiritual and visual journeys, which allowed me to roam beyond the four walls of these hospitals, had taught me how extremely important it is to live in the "NOW" and to get rid of life's many "distractions", which I too am guilty of having, in order to clearly chase down as many of your personal checkmarks as possible so that way when you do pass away you can "Die Empty" bringing no unfinished earthly business with you to the grave.

My friends, Your Imagination, Mental Imagery, and Affirmed Visualizations are the preview of your life's coming attractions. Everything ever created in this lifetime, and on this planet, is born twice. Once in the mind, and then once in the World. Protect your goals, dreams, and visions and make sure to always surround yourselves with people at your ambition level or above. We only "Get" on chance at life folks, this 'ain't no dress rehearsal.

Ladies & Gentlemen, I'm the Proud Son of the late great Mr. Gregorio Hierco Beltijar - (a Man of humble beginnings, who weathered every single storm that life threw at him, and was living proof that Dreams CAN come True) - Because of him, my loving mother, my supportive sister, & my brilliant god-son nephew I'm a believer in people. I'm a foolish dreamer, with my head forever in the clouds, whose thoughts have taken me to places where logic doesn't exist on route to returning and claiming victory over the Greatest adversity of my life. Being a believer in the power of visualization gives me the trusting ability to see people, or anything, for what they can become and not necessarily for where they're currently at.

If you're looking to get to that next level of personal achievement but don't know how to get there I invite you to visit my website at www.ThePositiveDrip.com and reach out to me via E'mail at ThePositiveDrip@hotmail.com to Book your Complimentary "30 minute" Coaching Session, with the code word "Relentless" typed into the Subject area, and Together we'll Crush adversity as we Start to climb, and eventually Conquer, your Mountains of perceived can'ts and paralyzing impossibilities. The time is Now to Step into "Your" personal "Greatness" and go after the things that you Want and Deserve. Know that I'm Looking forward to Speaking with You - "Tomorrow" 😋 .

~ About Dr. Nelson Beltijar ~
The Visionary

Dr. Nelson Beltijar, Entertaining International Motivational & Educational Speaker and Honorary Doctorate Graduate from the Cornerstone Christian University (CCU) in Christian Leadership & Business, is a Certified Life & Executive Business Coach, Physical Therapist, 3x Amazon # 1 International Bestselling Book Author, and Author of the "Accidental," yet, Globally Impactful Blog www.ThePositiveDrip.com.

He Considers Himself Fortunate to have had the ability to participate, struggle, fail, and excel in many personal endeavours, as well as team and individual sports & business ventures.

He feels truly blessed to have had coaches, teachers, instructors, mentors, teammates, friends, and family members who have always provided him with a positive environment to grow.

At the height of his professional career, he was faced with "***THE***" adversity of his life. As a result, Nelson will "lovingly" be the very first person to tell anyone, without a shadow of a doubt, that "Adversity" truly introduces a person to themselves.

...If you would like to "Convert" your life's greatest "Adversity" into your personal & professional "Advantage" within 90 days, via my signature program #SIG90x, I invite you to reach out to me at ThePositiveDrip@hotmail.com and type the word "Relentless90x" into the Subject heading area. Until then, know that I'm cheering you on and looking forward to connecting with you ... Tomorrow !!!

Contact Information

Jim Zias

EMAIL

JimZias@hotmail.com

WEBSITE

www.JimZias.com

FACEBOOK

https://www.facebook.com/profile.php?id=100090473241022

TIKTOK

JimZias

MAILING ADDRESS

Toronto, Ontario

Dr. John E. Gray

Professor of Positivity

Email

drjohn@EmpowermentMattersLLC.com

Phone

+ 1. 856. 244. 1233

Website

www.professorofpositivity.com

Facebook

@John E Gray

Twitter

@drofpositivity

Instagram

@professor_of_positivity

LinkedIn

@Dr. John E Gray

YouTube Channel

https://www.youtube.com/channel/UCdUVk8V0LqqbHTebF58GAYw

Briar Munro

Briar Munro Coaching

EMAIL

briarmunro@gmail.com

WEBSITE

www.briarmunro.com

INSTAGRAM

@briarmunro12

Aubrey Johnson

The Road to Rediscovery Podcast

EMAIL

roadtorediscoverypodcast@gmail.com

PHONE NUMBER

+1-513-373-0581

WEBSITE

www.road2rediscovery.com

FACEBOOK

https://www.facebook.com/R2RPodcast

TWITTER

https://twitter.com/R2RPodcast

INSTAGRAM

https://www.instagram.com/AJShark49

LINKEDIN

https://www.linkedin.com/in/aubreyjohnsonr2r/

YOUTUBE CHANNEL

https://www.youtube.com/channel/UCuCTQBQcU8RfgZl_WV9CepA

TikTok

@R2RPodcast

Mailing Address

108 Butler Street

Anna, TX, 75409

Ly Smith

UpCycle Coaching LLC

EMAIL

coach@upcyclecoaching.com

PHONE NUMBER

+1-775-583-8767

WEBSITE

www.UpCycleCoaching.com

FACEBOOK

https://www.facebook.com/ly.smith.speaker

INSTAGRAM

https://www.instagram.com/ly.smith.speaker

LINKEDIN

https://www.linkedin.com/in/ly-smith-speaker

MAILING ADDRESS

2015 Long Hollow Dr.
Reno, NV, 89521

Karl Davidson

Be Epic Coaching LTD

EMAIL

karldavidsondavitt@gmail.com

FACEBOOK

https://www.facebook.com/KarlDavidsonONE/

TWITTER

https://twitter.com/Karl_Dav

INSTAGRAM

https://www.instagram.com/followingkarldavidson

LINKEDIN

https://www.linkedin.com/in/karl-davidson-b-eng-nlpmp-qbe-54070b52/

TIKTOK

https://www.youtube.com/@karldavidson/

https://www.tiktok.com/@cashflowclubireland.Celbridge

Kildare, Leinster, 0000

Karan MacLaren
KM MIND BODY SPIRIT

EMAIL

kmmindbodyspirit@gmail.com

PHONE NUMBER

+1-647-781-6542

MAILING ADDRESS

Markdale, Ontario, N0C 1S0

Frankie Kington

The Wise Entrepreneur

EMAIL

frankie.lisafruitfulleaders@gmail.com

PHONE NUMBER

+4-474-543-5960

WEBSITE

www.frankiekington.com

FACEBOOK

www.facebook.com/empoweringyouthdevelopment

TWITTER

https://twitter.com/FrankieKington

INSTAGRAM

https://www.instagram.com/frankie_kington/

LINKEDIN

https://www.linkedin.com/in/frankie-kington-164299b8/

YOUTUBE CHANNEL

https://www.youtube.com/channel/UCTUDjgkwMWJitmAfCfINUMw

TikTok

https://www.tiktok.com/@frankiekington69

Mailing Address

8 McCall Walk Clayton

Manchester, Lancashire, M11 4EY

Master Tessa Gordon

Mamba Martial Arts

EMAIL

tessakicks@gmail.com

PHONE NUMBER

+1-917-601-5382

WEBSITE

www.mambamartialarts.com

Michael Clayborn

EMAIL

mtclayborn@yahoo.com

TWITTER

https://www.facebook.com/michaelandporsha.clayborn

LINKEDIN

https://www.instagram.com/michaelandporsha/

TIKTOK

https://www.youtube.com/watch?v=EnJ_eOtVpGw

Dawn Long

Dawn Long Coach

EMAIL

dawnlongempowermentcoach@gmail.com

PHONE NUMBER

+1-417-986-2543

WEBSITE

https://www.dawnlongcoach.com

FACEBOOK

https://www.facebook.com/YourTransformationJourney

INSTAGRAM

https://instagram.com/dawnlongcoach/

LINKEDIN

https://www.linkedin.com/in/dawnlong/

YOUTUBE CHANNEL

https://www.youtube.com/channel/UC6AE_PfvuUcHThDseXIMJXA

RELENTLESS
Empowering Stories of Overcoming Adversity

TikTok

@yourtransformationjourne

Mailing Address

84 Cook Hill Rd

Anderson, MO 64831

Flex Marks

Flex Training System

EMAIL

Flextrainingsystem@gmail.com

WEBSITE

https://freakmusclebuilding.com/

FACEBOOK

https://www.facebook.com/flex.marks

INSTAGRAM

https://www.instagram.com/flexmarks/

YOUTUBE CHANNEL

https://www.youtube.com/channel/UCP-t6YHsyxDMCV5hRliIoFg

Lindsay Cruz

EMAIL

lindsayanncruz@gmail.com

INSTAGRAM

@lindsayanncruz

Justin Smith

WEBSITE

www.justinbrennonsmith.com

LINKEDIN

https://www.linkedin.com/in/justinbrennonsmith/

Meaghan Tanaka

EMAIL

meaghantanaka@gmail.com

LINKEDIN

https://www.linkedin.com/in/meaghan-tanaka-4ab89925

MAILING ADDRESS

Toronto, ON

Tony Lynch

Memories of Us ᴸᵀᴰ Grief Support For Men

EMAIL

tolynch46@gmail.com

PHONE NUMBER

+1-970-599-9917

WEBSITE

www.memorieofus.org

www.globalgriefnetwork.com

FACEBOOK

Memories of us ltd/global grief network

INSTAGRAM

Mensgriefsupport

LINKEDIN

Tony Lynch / global grief network

YOUTUBE CHANNEL

https://www.youtube.com/@griefletstalkaboutit

RELENTLESS
Empowering Stories of Overcoming Adversity

MAILING ADDRESS

1305 Apt B
Loveland, Colorado 80537

Sid Owsley

D3 Global Enterprise

EMAIL

owsleysid@gmail.com

PHONE NUMBER

+1-240-936-1293

WEBSITE

www.sidowsley.com

FACEBOOK

https://www.facebook.com/sidney.owsley?mibextid=LQQJ4d

TWITTER

https://twitter.com/sidowsley?s=21&t=c7OOO-pYPGcboYsiHDkrGg

INSTAGRAM

https://twitter.com/sidowsley?s=21&t=c7OOO-pYPGcboYsiHDkrGg

LINKEDIN

https://www.linkedin.com/in/sid-owsley-b4993218

RELENTLESS

Empowering Stories of Overcoming Adversity

YOUTUBE CHANNEL

https://www.youtube.com/@SidOwsley

TIKTOK

https://www.tiktok.com/@sidowsley895?_t=8c9yaVFRA3G&_r=1

MAILING ADDRESS

5115 W Grace Ct.

Williamsburg, VA 23188

Benitha Samuel

THE BENNY EXPRESSION

EMAIL

benithasamueledemeka@gmail.com

TWITTER

https://web.facebook.com/thebennyexpressionshow

LINKEDIN

https://www.instagram.com/bennyexpression/

YOUTUBE CHANNEL

https://www.linkedin.com/in/benithasamuel/

TIKTOK

www.youtube.com/channel/UCMEYqUOiJMLKqEUEO5xmn2Q

La Toya Bond

Speaking Of Love Media Productions LLC

EMAIL

beautifultoy@me.com

WEBSITE

www.beautifultoy.net/speaking-of-love.html

FACEBOOK

https://www.facebook.com/speakingoflovepodcast

INSTAGRAM

@beautifulcreationsbytoy

YOUTUBE CHANNEL

https://youtube.com/@beautifultoy

TIKTOK

@beautifultoy

Dr. Nelson Beltijar, PhD, (h.c.)

The Positive Drip

EMAIL

ThePositiveDrip@hotmail.com

WEBSITE

www.ThePositiveDrip.com

FACEBOOK

https://www.facebook.com/nelson.beltijar/

YOUTUBE

https://www.youtube.com/@ThePositiveDrip

RELENTLESS
Empowering Stories of Overcoming Adversity

About the Project Manager,
WRITING CONSULTANT & CONTENT EDITOR

~ DR. ANGIE GRAY ~

Having had a love for reading and writing for as long as she can remember, Dr. Angie Gray is truly operating under her umbrella of purpose. Over the years she has won many distinctive awards for her gift of writing. Her accolades go back as far as elementary school when she wrote poetry and traveled throughout her home state of New Jersey to share writing through poetry recitations to churches, associations, and civic organizations.

As the winner of such prestigious awards as the Gannett National Journalism Award and the KYW News Radio Award, Angie's writing skills have served her well. Her writing career has led her to the path of *Bestselling Author* and *International Bestselling Author*, sealing her respect and credentials within the world of writing.

Dr. Gray's degree in Communications and multi-decade career in education has solidified a strong foundation on which to build her project management and publishing ventures to further serve the writing community and the universe-at-large. She attributes her success and achievements to her divine purpose and God-given gifts and talents.

Angie is the co-founder of **Onyx Expressions, LLC** and the Amazon Bestselling Author of **Back From The Brink: The Blessing Of A Near-Death**

Dr. Nelson Beltijar, Visionary Author

Experience, contributing author of the Amazon International Bestseller, ***The Women of the Power Voice*** and the book series, ***One Good Sip at a Time.***

Connect With Our Writing Consultant Dr. Angie Gray

Email
drangie@EmpowermentMattersLLC.com

Phone
+ 1. 856. 270. 8883

Website
www.DrAngieGray.com

Facebook
https://www.facebook.com/DrAngieGray

Twitter
https://twitter.com/DrAngieGray

Instagram
https://www.instagram.com/drangiegray4/

LinkedIn
https://www.linkedin.com/in/dr-angie-gray/

YouTube
https://www.youtube.com/channel/UCEuSQbswnZ-A8CY22FnOKuQ

Mailing Address
Empowerment Matters, LLC
% Dr. Angie Gray
P.O. Box 84
Sicklerville, NJ 08081

About The Publisher

Onyx Expressions Publishing is a full-service publishing company that seeks to join aspiring authors on their journey to becoming published authors. The mission of *Onyx Expressions* is to breathe life into the divine voice, purpose, and legacy of individuals desiring to enhance their life's work, significance, and influence through sharing the author's story through writing. Realizing that one's story is their true wealth, *Onyx Expressions* helps authors to deliver their story in a way that is healing and hope-filled for their readers; one story, one book, and one life at a time.

Embracing the art, science, and business of writing, *Onyx Expressions* supports both novice and experienced authors who are serious about their craft and in pursuit of living the best version of themselves. This publishing organization proudly produces quality publication of books, eBooks, and speeches as the springboard for entrepreneurial endeavors their clients engage as a means to encourage, inspire, and empower others.

Onyx Expressions maintains a proven track record of successful publication projects including; anthologies, eBooks, books, courses, promotional launches, speeches, and writing retreats. Excellence in editing, cover design, formatting, proofreading, coaching, writing assistance, accountability, ghostwriting, marketing & promotion, and consultation are among the services *Onyx Expressions* consistently delivers for their clients.

Manufactured by Amazon.ca
Bolton, ON

35201425R00144